First World War
and Army of Occupation
War Diary
France, Belgium and Germany

40 DIVISION
119 Infantry Brigade
East Lancashire Regiment
13th Battalion
10 June 1918 - 30 April 1919

WO95/2606/2

The Naval & Military Press Ltd
www.nmarchive.com
Published in association with The National Archives

Published by

The Naval & Military Press Ltd

Unit 10 Ridgewood Industrial Park,

Uckfield, East Sussex,

TN22 5QE England

Tel: +44 (0) 1825 749494

www.naval-military-press.com

www.nmarchive.com

This diary has been reprinted in facsimile from the original. Any imperfections are inevitably reproduced and the quality may fall short of modern type and cartographic standards.

© **Crown Copyright**
Images reproduced by permission of The National Archives, London, England, 2015.

Contents

Document type	Place/Title	Date From	Date To
Heading	WO95/2606/2 13 Battalion East Lancashire Regiment		
Heading	40th Division 119th Infy Bde 13th Bn East Lancs Regt Jun 1918-Apr 1919 Formed on France June 1918		
Heading	War Diary June 1918 13th East Lanc. Vol I		
War Diary	Etaples	10/06/1918	10/06/1918
War Diary	Middel Strate	11/06/1918	15/06/1918
War Diary	Nieurlet	16/06/1918	23/06/1918
War Diary	V. 13. D. II.	24/06/1918	30/06/1918
War Diary	U 18 d 9.5	30/06/1918	30/06/1918
War Diary	V 13 D 11	01/07/1918	06/07/1918
War Diary	V 27 To V 17	07/07/1918	09/07/1918
War Diary	V 13 D 11	13/07/1918	16/07/1918
War Diary	V 24	17/07/1918	17/07/1918
War Diary	E 3. C. 1.8	18/07/1918	27/07/1918
War Diary	V 24 Central	27/07/1918	30/07/1918
War Diary	V 13 d 1.1.	31/07/1918	31/07/1918
Operation(al) Order(s)	Operation Order No. 2 by Lt. Col R.I.B. Johnson D.S.O.	14/07/1918	14/07/1918
Operation(al) Order(s)	Operation Order No. 2	14/07/1918	14/07/1918
Operation(al) Order(s)	Operation Order No. 2 By H.M. R.I.H. Johnson D.S.O.	14/07/1918	14/07/1918
Heading	War Diary		
Operation(al) Order(s)	Operation Order No. 3 by Lt. Col. R.I.B. Johnson. D.S.O.	17/07/1918	17/07/1918
Heading	Operation Order		
Operation(al) Order(s)	Operation Order by Lt. Col. R.I.B. Johnson D.S.O. Comdg 13th East Lancs Regt.	17/07/1918	17/07/1918
Operation(al) Order(s)	Operation Order No. 4 by Lt. Col. R.I.B. Johnson. D.S.O.	21/07/1918	21/07/1918
Operation(al) Order(s)	Operation Order No. 4 by Lt. Col. R.B. Johnson. D.S.O.	21/07/1918	21/07/1918
Miscellaneous	Warning Notice.	23/07/1918	23/07/1918
Miscellaneous	Warning Notice No 5	23/07/1918	23/07/1918
Operation(al) Order(s)	Operation Order. No. 6 by Lt Col R.I.B. Johnson D.S.O.	21/07/1918	21/07/1918
Operation(al) Order(s)	Operation Order No. 6 by Lt Col R.I.B. Johnson D.S.O.	26/07/1918	26/07/1918
Operation(al) Order(s)	Operation Order No. 7 by Lt. Col. R.I.B. Johnson D.S.O.	29/07/1918	29/07/1918
Heading	War Diary 13th East Lancashire Rgt August 1918 Vol 3		
War Diary	V 13 d 11	01/08/1918	12/08/1918
War Diary	Lumbres	13/08/1918	16/08/1918
War Diary	V 13 d 11.	17/08/1918	23/08/1918
War Diary	Vieux Berquin	23/08/1918	25/08/1918
War Diary	Vieux Berquin Sector	26/08/1918	30/08/1918
War Diary	Le Tir Anglais	30/08/1918	30/08/1918
Operation(al) Order(s)	Operation Order No. 12	11/08/1918	11/08/1918
Miscellaneous	13th. East Lancashire Rgt. Office Scheme	19/08/1918	19/08/1918
Operation(al) Order(s)	Operation Order No. 7 by Lt. Col. R.B. Johnson D.S.O. Commdg 13th East Lancs Regt	22/08/1918	22/08/1918
Operation(al) Order(s)	13 Bn East Lanchashire Rgt. Operation Order No. 8	28/09/1915	28/09/1915

Type	Description	Start	End
Operation(al) Order(s)	Operation Order No. 13 by Major S. Tabor Commanding	29/08/1918	29/08/1918
War Diary	Le Tir Anglais	01/09/1918	02/09/1918
War Diary	Pont Wemeau	03/09/1918	03/09/1918
War Diary	Steenwerck	04/09/1918	05/09/1918
War Diary	Nieppe Sector	06/09/1918	13/09/1918
War Diary	Pont Wemeau	13/09/1918	21/09/1918
War Diary	Hazebrouck	22/09/1918	25/09/1918
War Diary	B.5. D 3.2	26/09/1918	29/09/1918
War Diary	B.6.C. 55 2.4.	30/09/1918	30/09/1918
Operation(al) Order(s)	Operation Order No. 13 by Major. S. Tabor Commdg 13th East Lancs Regt.	02/09/1918	02/09/1918
Operation(al) Order(s)	Operation Order No 15 by Major S. Tabor	06/09/1918	06/09/1918
Miscellaneous	Orders O.C. D Coy. T.J. 57.	07/09/1918	07/09/1918
Miscellaneous	Orders O.C. A Coy. T.J. 59	07/09/1918	07/09/1918
Miscellaneous	Report On Major Operation of Sept 7th 1918	07/09/1918	07/09/1918
Miscellaneous	Relief Order	08/09/1918	08/09/1918
Operation(al) Order(s)	Operation Order No. 17 By Lt. Col B.B. Johnson D.S.O. Commanding 13 Bn East Lancs Regt.	12/09/1918	12/09/1918
Operation(al) Order(s)	Operation Order No 14 by Major S. Tabor Commanding 5th Bn East Lancs Regt.	14/09/1918	14/09/1918
Operation(al) Order(s)	Operation Orders No 13 Major N.W.D. Cox. Comdg 13th E. Lancs. Regt.	20/09/1918	20/09/1918
Operation(al) Order(s)	Operation Order No 20 Lt. Col. Johnson D.S.O. Cmdg 13th East Lancs. Rgt.		
Heading	War Diary 13th E Lancashire Regt Month Of October Vol 5		
War Diary	Nieppe Area Armen Tiers	01/10/1918	04/10/1918
War Diary	Armentiers	05/10/1918	05/10/1918
War Diary	Nippon Bend	06/10/1918	13/10/1918
War Diary	A 10a 7095	14/10/1918	19/10/1918
War Diary	J.I.B.	19/10/1918	23/10/1918
War Diary	Bondues	24/10/1918	25/10/1918
War Diary	Roubaix	26/10/1918	27/10/1918
War Diary	Croix	27/10/1918	27/10/1918
War Diary	Wattrelos	28/10/1918	31/10/1918
Operation(al) Order(s)	Operation Order. 21 by Major E O'Connor.	03/10/1918	03/10/1918
Operation(al) Order(s)	Operation Order No 28 by Lt Coy R.J. Andrews D.S.O.M.C.		
Operation(al) Order(s)	Operation Order No 28 by Lt Col R.J. Andrews D.S.O. M.C.		
Operation(al) Order(s)	Operation Orders 21 by Major E O'Connor.	03/10/1918	03/10/1918
Operation(al) Order(s)	13th East Lancs Rgt Operation Order No 21	06/10/1918	06/10/1918
Operation(al) Order(s)	Operation Orders No. 22 by Lt. Col R.J. Andrews D.S.O. M.C., Cmdg 13th Bn East Lancs Rgt.	11/10/1918	11/10/1918
Operation(al) Order(s)	Operation Order No 22 by Lt Col R.J. Andrews. D.S.O. M.C. Cmdg. 13th Bn. East Lancs. Regt.	11/10/1918	11/10/1918
Miscellaneous	Distribution List		
Operation(al) Order(s)	Operation Order 13	11/10/1918	11/10/1918
Miscellaneous	Distribution List.		
Operation(al) Order(s)	Operation Order No. 13	16/10/1918	16/10/1918
Miscellaneous	Distribution List.		
Operation(al) Order(s)	Operation Order No 24 By Lt Col. R.G.Andreues. D.S.O. M.C. Commdg 13th East James Regt	17/10/1918	17/10/1918
Miscellaneous	Distribution List.		
Operation(al) Order(s)	Operation Order No 24		

Miscellaneous	Distribution List.		
Operation(al) Order(s)	Operation Order No. 25 by Lt. Col. R.J. Andrews D.S.O., M.C. Commdg. 13th East Lancs. Regt.	13/10/1918	13/10/1918
Miscellaneous	Distribution List		
Operation(al) Order(s)	Operation Order No. 25 by Lt Col. R.J. Andrews D.S.O., M.C. Commdg 13th East. James. Regt.	18/10/1915	18/10/1915
Miscellaneous	Distribution List.		
Operation(al) Order(s)	Operation Order No 26 by Lt Col R.J. Andrews D.S.O. MC.	23/10/1918	23/10/1918
Miscellaneous	A Of T		
Operation(al) Order(s)	Operation Orders by Lt Col R.J. Andrews D.S.O. M.C	23/10/1918	23/10/1918
Operation(al) Order(s)	Operation Orders No 27 by Lt Col R.G Andrews D.S.O., M.C. Commdg. 13 East Lancs Regt.	25/10/1918	25/10/1918
Miscellaneous	Operation Orders No 27 by. Lt Col R.J. Andrews D.S.O., M.C. Comdg 13th Bn East Lancashire Regt	25/10/1918	25/10/1918
Miscellaneous	Adj		
Heading	War Diary Of 13th Bn East Lancashire Regiment. Month Of November 1918 Vol 6		
War Diary	Leers Nord	01/11/1918	03/11/1918
War Diary	Pecq To	04/11/1918	10/11/1918
War Diary	Pecq Operation	05/11/1918	11/11/1918
War Diary	Herrines	12/11/1918	16/11/1918
Heading	13th East Lancs Regt War Diary From 1st December 1918 To 31st December 1918 Vol 7		
War Diary	Croix	01/12/1918	31/01/1919
Heading	War Diary 13th Bn. East Lancashire Rgt. Volume IX Feby 1919		
War Diary	Croix	01/01/1919	28/01/1919
Heading	13th Bn East Lancs Regt. Vol 10 War Diary Volume X For Month Of March 1919		
War Diary	Croix.	01/03/1919	31/03/1919
Miscellaneous	O/C Record Section British Troops In France	10/05/1919	10/05/1919
War Diary	Croix.	01/04/1919	30/04/1919
Miscellaneous	14. XII. 24		
Miscellaneous	Blandford Lodge. Whiteknights, Reading.	24/01/1915	24/01/1915
Miscellaneous	Albemarle Court Hotel.	12/09/1927	12/09/1927
Miscellaneous	History Of 13th. Bn The East Lancashire Regiment.		

WO95/2606/2
13 Battalion East Lancashire Regiment

40TH DIVISION
119TH INFY BDE

13TH BN EAST LANCS REGT

JUN 1918-APR 1919

Formed in France June 1918

Army Form C. 2118.

WAR DIARY
or
INTELLIGENCE SUMMARY.
(Erase heading not required.)

Instructions regarding War Diaries and Intelligence Summaries are contained in F. S. Regs., Part II. and the Staff Manual respectively. Title pages will be prepared in manuscript.

Place	Date	Hour	Summary of Events and Information	Remarks and references to Appendices
ETAPLES	10.6.18	6 AM	First formation of Bn. H.Q. Personnel only (Comdg. Officer Col. W. HODSON D.S.O. M.C. Clerks Regtl. 1st in command Lieut. S. TABOR 3rd Bedfordshire Regt. 2nd in Command Capt. J.W. STOPFORD Adjutant 4th Bn. Bedfordshire Regt. 2nd Lieut. A. PATERKIN 10th Sherwood Foresters Lt & Qr M. G.T. CLAPHAM Lee Corpl Quartermaster, 2nd Lieut W KNIGHT O/C Bn. Orderly Officer, Lieut MORRIS 1st York & Lancs Signalling Officer, Lieut STANNING Durham L.I. Transport Officer and 104 Other ranks entrained at Etaples at 7am. arr. at WATTEN (RENSON marched to MIDDEL STAT KERKERZEELE arrived Regt HAZEBROUCK 5.32 D.S.I. Situation followed await A3 G.O. canon 2 in a Commander reporting to O/C 110th Inf Bde 1 with his Brigade Major Bn. OK'd on as N05 garrison Bn	
MIDDEL STRATE	11.6.18		Reorganisation of B.N. allotted to 13th Q.v. Bn 2nd East Lancashire R.G.F. CO's writing his Lieut Col Noisson accompanied a Diary & from 20th 7th Div. forward (? ....?.....)	G.
do	12.6.18	3 PM	Received command	G.
			This diary P.T.Y.B.F. (handwriting unclear) up (illegible)	G.

Army Form C. 2118.

WAR DIARY
or
INTELLIGENCE SUMMARY.
(Erase heading not required.)

Instructions regarding War Diaries and Intelligence Summaries are contained in F. S. Regs., Part II. and the Staff Manual respectively. Title pages will be prepared in manuscript.

Place	Date	Hour	Summary of Events and Information	Remarks and references to Appendices
MIDDEL STRAETE	13.6.18		Bros Relief. Bombing and P.T. L.G.S. Classes and Drums fires.	G.
	14.6.18		Box respirals elementary and testing by N.C.O. H.B. of battn at NIEUVERDINGH	G.
	15.6.18		Proceeded to NIEURLET near ST OMER by route march to field	G.
		11 AM	B.N transferred to 119th BDE	
NIEURLET	16.6.18	9 AM	Major TABOR (car ST POPAM (ADV) and Lieut Morris proceeded to LA BREARDE. by lorry to reconnoitre portion of West Hazebrouck line allotted to the B.N. from Y.II d.4.0 (inclusive) to Y.6.a.8.2 (inclusive) (Ref) Belgium Sheet 27 S.E. 2000	G.
do	16.6.18	8 PM	17 Officers and 760 O.R. arrived from Labour Boys at WATTEN to form 4 coys.	G.
do	17.6.18	11 AM	B.N inspection by Brigadier-General B.Ch. Commander	
		2.20 pm	B.N inspection by Div. Gen. Ponsonby Div. Commander. H.Q.2nd Division	
		4 pm	Lieut Colonel R.I.B. JOHNSON, D.S.O. ROYAL WELSH FUS. took over command.	G.
do	18.6.18		B.N training, Squad drill, Musketry and Specialist training	G.

WAR DIARY or INTELLIGENCE SUMMARY

Army Form C. 2118.

Place	Date	Hour	Summary of Events and Information	Remarks and references to Appendices
NIEURLET	19.6.18		Training, Squad drill, Platoon drill and Musketry. Lewis Gun, Lewis Gun Officer & Mess Kelly, Lewis Gun & Lig Officers and Lewis went 4 Coy Commanders, Transport Officer & Lig Officers and Lewis N.C.Os reconnoitred position in West Hazebrouck line. V.11. C.94 to V8. C.78. V.10 Central on the night to a line running through W7.B.37 – V.12.B.00.99 – V.6.C.05 – V.5 Central.	—
		2.30pm	119 & Bde inspected by D.A.G. Bde formed up in close column at Contamine. B Coy General. A and B Coy gathered at ST MOMELIN. Lewis Gunners under instruction on No 15 frieze on ranges remainder Bn Musketry P.T. and P.T. drill	—
	20.6.18			—
do.	21.6.18	9am	A Coy fired on range Shooting Practice 137 O.R.firers average 14.5 pairs of B.104 fired. Firing Drifted as Chinese labour refused to work in vicinity	—
			B Coy gathered ST MOMELIN	—
do	22.6.18	9-5	R.119 & Bde Route march to CINQ RUES and return. 17. O.R. fell out.	—
do	23.6.18	7.30 AM	Right-half Bn. H.Q. marched to ST OMER via NIEURRLET INEY Road entrained at 9.30 AM delivered at U.19.A.11. marched to V.13.D.1.1	—

WAR DIARY or INTELLIGENCE SUMMARY

Army Form C. 2118.

Place	Date	Hour	Summary of Events and Information	Remarks and references to Appendices
NIEURLET	23.6	10.30 am	Left Ref Bn proceeded by route march and arrived at H.Q. V.13.D.1.1. Sheet 27 Belgium pour l' France Zone at 2.30 pm. Bn Billeted.	L.1.
V.13.D.1.1.	24.6		Cleaned up & inspection instead. 9.6.12H.00 all Coys for drill. Platoon and Musketry. B Coy on range in afternoon practice (Nothing owing to heavy rain)	L.1.
do	25.6	10 AM	Bn marched to LA BRÉARDE and occupied PP6 and line of resistance in WEST HAZEBROUCK LINE, Outpost Coys A and B. C and D in support Bn H.Q. at V.5.C.8.4. Outposts were from V.18.C.10.75 to W.7.A.2.9. C Coy at V.11.A. D Coy V.5.C. Bn returned to billets at V.13.D.1.1.	L.1.
do	26.6		Training. Musketry rapid loading, Outpost and Scheme. D Coy on range. Inspection by M.O. 7.6. Coy Specialist training.	L.1.
do	27.6		Training. Musketry, Platoon drill, Outpost, Mass scheme, Initiative. 7.A and B Coys by M.O. and Specialists training. A Coy on Range on New Range at V.12.d.7.4. 27.S.W.	L.1.

Army Form C. 2118.

WAR DIARY
or
INTELLIGENCE SUMMARY.
(Erase heading not required.)

Place	Date	Hour	Summary of Events and Information	Remarks and references to Appendices
	1918			
V.13 d.1.1.	26.6		Training. Musketry. Platoon drill. P.T. Outposts. D.Coy digging on new range. Football match Officers & N.C.Os Officers won 4-1. L.O. reconnoitred W. HAZEBROUCK line with Signalling Officer	S.
	29.6		Training. New Rosy. B. Coy on range. A Coy digging on new range. Platoon drill. Outposts. Inspecting Arms of A Coy by Bde Armourer Sergt. D Coy Route march.	S.
	30.6	10 am	Church Parade. 119 Bde, 13th Royal Innishilling Fus. and 13th East Lancs. Football match 119 Bde H.Q. V 13 E. Lancs. Bde won 3-2. A Coy taken at HONDEGHEM	S.
U18 d.9.5				

R. B. Ingram.
Lieut Colonel
Commanding
13th (G.B) East Lancashire Regt

Army Form C. 2118.

13 E Lane Vol 1

WAR DIARY
or
INTELLIGENCE SUMMARY.
(Erase heading not required.)

Instructions regarding War Diaries and Intelligence Summaries are contained in F. S. Regs., Part II. and the Staff Manual respectively. Title pages will be prepared in manuscript.

Place	Date	Hour	Summary of Events and Information	Remarks and references to Appendices
1918				
July	V13a4 1/7/18	9 am	"B" Coy bathed at Hondeghem. B" inspection by C.O. in cattle new formation Close column of companies. Training (Musketry) Platoon drill, P.T. Lecture to Senior officers and Coy Commanders on Gas at H.Q. R Soms Two	R.
	2.7.10	7-30	Saluting and Coy respirator drill	
		9 am	C.O.'s inspection of "B" in fighting order	
		8-15 pm	Inspection of 119th Bde by F.M. H.R.H. The Duke of Connaught at V27 a 17 c.6.9. in attendance Genl Plumer Lieut Genl de Lisle and Staff	R.
		6 pm	Lecture by C.O. to all officers, Subjects Cadres Working party on new range proposed by D. Coy	3
	3.7.16	6.45 am	Training, Gas drill, machinery in mass. Musketry Platoon and Company formation training, Muskery for all Coys, P.T. and inclination training 2nd in Command reconnoitred position of reserve line thur	2
			HAZEWINDE 1000 from V27 a.4.0. running N.E. V.16.d.12.60 "B" Coy bathed at HONDEGHEM	R.

Army Form C. 2118.

WAR DIARY
or
INTELLIGENCE SUMMARY.
(Erase heading not required.)

Instructions regarding War Diaries and Intelligence Summaries are contained in F. S. Regs. Part II. and the Staff Manual respectively. Title pages will be prepared in manuscript.

Place	Date	Hour	Summary of Events and Information	Remarks and references to Appendices
V13 d 11 #7f	4.7.18		Appreciation. H.R.H. The Duke of Connaught was pleased to express to the Major General ij Division his great appreciation of the appearance of the 119th Inf Bde yesterday, he wished all ranks to be informed. Div order of the day dated 3-7-16	
		9AM	"A" Coy inoculated. "B" Coy on range 8AM to 1PM. remainder of B Coy P.T. Musketry instruction of Lewis and rapid loading. "D" Coy hoisting of arms.	G.
"		5.7.18 9am	"A" Bn & C. Cos river. Mens kits P.T. P.N drill	
		12noon	B Coy bathed in afternoon. Specialist training	
		2f	A and C Coy then route march in fighting order	
		3-30f	D Coy working party on the range.	G.
		6.7.16 9am	A Coy Inspection of arms by Armourer. Physical instruction by M.O after 48 hours inoculation. B Coy on P.N working on range. B. C. and D Coys Coys every morning	G.

Army Form C. 2118.

WAR DIARY
or
INTELLIGENCE SUMMARY.
(Erase heading not required.)

Place	Date	Hour	Summary of Events and Information	Remarks and references to Appendices
V.27 to V.17	7.7.16	12 Noon	The Bn relieved the 13th R. Irish Rif in the EAST HAZEBROUCK LINE S.West HAZEBRINDE 2000. Coys marched independently to Bn. H.Q. R. Irish arriving at 9.30 A.M. "A" Coy No. 1 Cellar Coy, B. Coy No. 2 Outpost on right. C. Coy in support to "A" D. Coy in support to B Coy. Bn H.Q. situated at V.15 a 90.05. Relief carried out by 1.15 p.m.	G.
	8.7.16	7 A.M.	Commanding Officer and I'g Officer went round line. Relieved at 9.30 A.M. C and D Coys provided working parties of 100 men each. On going under R.E. supervision on trench digging, two parties totalling parties of 40 each on burying cable. "B" Co. Comm'd went round line and same time of Coys came by 2nd in Command. Weather fine.	G.
	9.7.16	2 P.M.	Command'g Officer went round line in afternoon. Wet by Coys as in previous day. Bn. carried out its ordinary relief. B relieved A. D relieved B. Relief carried out by night and completed by 11.15 p.m.	G.

Army Form C. 2118.

WAR DIARY
or
INTELLIGENCE SUMMARY.
(Erase heading not required.)

Instructions regarding War Diaries and Intelligence Summaries are contained in F. S. Regs., Part II. and the Staff Manual respectively. Title pages will be prepared in manuscript.

Place	Date	Hour	Summary of Events and Information	Remarks and references to Appendices
V.27.b V.17	7.7.18	12 Noon	The Bn relieved the 13th R. Irish Regt in the EAST HAZEBROUCK LINE Sheet HAZEBRUNDE 20.000. Bays marched into billets Coy H.Q. B Irish arriving at 9.30 A.M. "A" Coy No 1 Cooker Coy. B Coy No 2 Cooker on left. C Coy in Support to "A". D Coy in Support to B Coy. B.N.H.Q. Situated at V.15.a.90.00. Relief (on's a/c by 1.15 p.m.)	G.
"	8.7.16	7 AM	Commanding Officer and Lg Officer went round line relieved at 9.30 A.M. C and D Coys provided working parties of 100 men each on 'going under' R.E. Supervision on French digging, two hours lifts. Working parties of 40 men on being 2nd in Command went round men came of reinc rainer by NIGHT. Weather fine.	G.
"	9.7.16	2 PM	Command'g Officer went round line in afternoon. Relief by Coys as for previous day. B.n. Casualties nil. Villa Foubourg relief C relieved A. D relieved B. relief carried out by night and completed by 11.15 P.m.	G.

WAR DIARY or INTELLIGENCE SUMMARY

Army Form C. 2118.

Place	Date	Hour	Summary of Events and Information	Remarks and references to Appendices
V.10.d.1.1	12/7/18	5:30 pm	The Commanding Officer awarded three Last Turned out Teams on the Transport after their Sports competition.	S.
"	14/7/18	9:30 am	Church Parade. In afternoon two Companies on range.	S.
"	14/7/18		C and D. Coys. Gas Test at Box H.Q. to all Coys.	S.
"	15/7/18		Practice Concentration in the West Hazebrouck area by the 119th	O.O.G.2.
			Bn. with application taken over for the scheme of defence.	
			Bn. moved off at 6.40 a.m. Bde Commander went round	B.
			area. Bn. returned to billets by 5-15 p.m.	
	16/7/18	7 pm	A. Coy on Range Practice was interfered with by heavy rain	
		9.30 am	C. Coy on Range after returning by Armourer Serj.	
			B. Coy. Gas Saluting Musketry Box/any Drill rapid loading	
			and on the range in afternoon 1 to 5 pm	
			D. Coy Gas PsT Musketry Loy drice Rifle inspection by Armourer S.	S.
			Specialists Training L.G.s on Range 5 to 7 pm	
V.24	17.7.18		The Bn. went into Western and relieved the 2nd Bn. K.O.S.B. at V.24 D.4.8 5.7½	O.O. No.B
			Infantry Bde. Transport moved to V.20.a.5.9.	

WAR DIARY
or
INTELLIGENCE SUMMARY.
(Erase heading not required.)

Army Form C. 2118.

Place	Date	Hour	Summary of Events and Information	Remarks and references to Appendices
E.3.C.1.8	18/7/18	7.30 pm	The Bn relieved the 2nd Bn S.W. B in trench posn. at E.10.D.75. (Casualties 1 killed & 1 wounded by Phos fire	O.O. No
"	19/7/18		Bn found working parties improving the support line. One Other Officer one civilian B Coy in conjunction with 9th Div had METEREN Bn in front line 13th R Innis Fus Coy zero 2 Pressures belonging to the 95th M.I.R at F.4.B.9.9.6 wounded were sent to the G.O.C.	
		9am	G.O. visited Front 18.C.4.6	
		10pm	G.O. visited D.Coy. 2nd in forward near normal Bn line 6.7 Coy.	
"	20.7.18		Bn found working parties improving front line trenches. One Officer R.E. Supervision 2nd in forward near Bond line at Pozzo b. 3.15 AM Coy Reserves and Pn/ Caren Reserves existed front line 10.7.18 R INNIS FUS to reconnoitre Bn posn.	
	21.7.18		Working parties found by all Coys. General improvement & development of each Coy recommended patrols of Front Bn.	
	22.7.18		Bn relieved 13th Bn R.INNIS FUS in the front line E.11.D.6.3– E.11.B.4.6 STRAZEELE sheet 2000. A Coy in right front posn. D Coy left front posn. Hd qtrs 2 P.N.S of C. Coy B Coy in support. C.A. C. Coy Coy 2 P'Cs.	O.O. N104

WAR DIARY
or
INTELLIGENCE SUMMARY.

(Erase heading not required.)

Army Form C. 2118.

Place	Date	Hour	Summary of Events and Information	Remarks and references to Appendices
	22.7.18 and 23.7.18		in support to D/Coy. The Bn held an outpost position A/Coy holding 3 posts Nos 1-3 with 1 Pn in immediate support. D/Coy holding 4 posts Nos 4-7 with 2 Pns of C/Coy in support. Relief completed by 3.30 A.M. Reliefs were attempted for front posts on ration dumps and carried to front posts by 1/Os in support. Active patrolling was carried out by front Coys. 2nd Lieut J.N. ROBINSON knew a Patrol	
	24.7.18		B.M. on night of 23rd Artillery preparation carried out against enemy posts on B.17.c and B.18.A party returned no identification.	
		2 A.M.	400 gas lachrymose fires on CELERY COPSE by No2 Special Coy Warning orders No 5 to carry out this in was necessary to withdraw the 2 front Coys. This was successfully carried out and the posts re-occupied by 2.20 a.m.	
	25.7.18		D/Coy captured 2 prisoners belonging to the 96 R.I.R. both belonged to the 1919 class and were four Germans. They had only had 3 months training. Their battalion had been on rest with us HAMBURG and has been 3 weeks in the line. Active patrolling was carried out throughout the Sector.	

WAR DIARY
or
INTELLIGENCE SUMMARY.
(Erase heading not required.)

Army Form C. 2118.

Place	Date	Hour	Summary of Events and Information	Remarks and references to Appendices
	25/26/9/16	11.30 P.M.	No 8 Post of A'Coy came over a raid. This objective being an enemy M.G. post at E.12.C.15.20 when within 20 yds they sighted the position which appeared to be empty the enemy having placed his guns on the flanks. 2nd Lieut A. LEE 1 Sergt and 12 men rushed the party, 2nd Lieut LEE on putting out that they were covered bring flanking fire ordered his party to withdraw. This was successfully carried out without loss. Lieut MASON A.I.F. and his Canadian Corporal who came out near the patrol to see how the attack was progressing were unfortunately killed. 2nd Lieut LEE took his Sergt and 3 men back and successfully brought back their bodies to our own lines. Action Casualty 2nd Lieut Pt.	
	26/27/9/16		The Bn was relieved in the line by the 12th & 18th North STAFFS. relief was successfully carried out and complete by 1.30 A.M. On the 27th B Bn went into Bde reserve at Vacher where they relieved the 13th R. INNIS. FUS who went into support at V.3.4.V.10 The Bn marched to wave by Pms Transports being used on this relief.	OO no 6

A6945 Wt. W1422/M1160 350,000 12/16 D. D. & L. Forms/C./2118/14.

Army Form C. 2118.

WAR DIARY
or
INTELLIGENCE SUMMARY.
(Erase heading not required.)

Place	Date	Hour	Summary of Events and Information	Remarks and references to Appendices
			During the B'n's tour in the front line they were attached to the 1st Australian Division, who placed at our disposal 1 Officer and 4 N.C.O.s per Coy. these Officers and N.C.O.s were invaluable in instructing both Officers and Men in their duties.	S.
24 October 7/11/18			A Bomb & Lewis Gun Gather working parties and fatigues were found by the B'n, working party no employed on BARRE-CAESTRE Cable trench and troops on duty in HAZEBROUCK.	
do		9.30 am	C.O. held a Conference at Bn. H.Q. and discussed the B & S. Coys duty founding out certain points which He was to return to remedy, on the whole he was satisfied with the B'n's work, Bn H.Q. has been having the not enough attention has been paid to messaging the Coys and wiring. Total B'n Casualties during tour Nil Offs ORs and Promoted 1 OR Wounded 2 H.O.R. 21 ORs	S.
do	28/7/18		B'n employed on Guards and carrying Cable trench.	

Army Form C. 2118.

WAR DIARY
or
INTELLIGENCE SUMMARY.
(Erase heading not required.)

Instructions regarding War Diaries and Intelligence Summaries are contained in F. S. Regs., Part II. and the Staff Manual respectively. Title pages will be prepared in manuscript.

Place	Date	Hour	Summary of Events and Information	Remarks and references to Appendices
V.24/central	29.7.18		Bn employed on grounds and digging cable trench	Eg
"	30.7.18		Bn relieved by the 23rd Bn CHESHIRE REGT relief complete after grounds were relieved in the afternoon by 4 pm. Bn moved to camp at	QG No 7 Eg
V.13 d.1.1	31.7.18	5.30 pm	Bn moved back to their old camps at V.13 d.1.1 and relieved the Bn Lancashire Fusiliers	Eg

R B Johnson
Lieut Colonel
Commanding 13th Bn East Lancashire Regt

SECRET   Operation Orders **No 2** Copy
24.7.18   by Lt. Col. R.A.B. Johnson D.S.O.
_____

1. There will be a practice manning of the WEST HAZEBROUCK line to-morrow.

2. The 13th East Lancs Regt will pass V.P. at S.1. at 7am. and will march on their markers on the Bn. Parade Ground at 6.15 am. They will be in position in the line at 10 am. Breakfasts at 5 am.

3. Troops will remain in position until further orders are sent by Bde. H.Qrs.

4. Dress, fighting order, haversack rations will be carried, dinners on return.

5. 2 Lt. WEEKS will report to a Bde. Staff Officer at U.11a.55 and will leave Bn. HQrs at 6.30am.

6. One N.C.O. and 4 men of "A" Coy, already detailed will report at Bde HQrs R.31d.5.7

7. Details left out in accordance with instructions already given i.e.
   R.Q.M.S.   4 C.Q.M.S.   Pioneer Sgt.   C.S.M. Turner
   C.S.M. "D" Coy   5 Shoemakers   4 Pioneers   Cpl. McConnell
   Master Cook   4 Tailors   Sgt. Drummer   Storeman
   8 Coy. Cooks   1. O.R. Clerk   Armr Sgt   Butcher
   1. Sanitary man   1. Post Cpl   Assistant   1. Mess Servant
   2 Runners   1. Servant   (H.Qrs)

8. One limber will march with Lewis Guns ammunition.

9. The remaining first line transport will carry the Batt. reserve S.A.A. there, afterwards returning to O.T.L. Central.

SECRET OPERATION ORDER No 2.
(Continued)

10. The M.G. cart will go with Batt HQrs and unload afterwards returning with the other transport.

11. Water if wanted will be drawn from the dump, one water cart will go with Batt. HQ to refill tins, the other water cart going with transport.

12. On reaching V 10 C 74 Coys will be marched independantly to their respective Sectors & man the posts and trenches as soon as possible, reporting to Batt HQ when they are in position. "A" Coy will get into touch with R. Innis Fus and "B" Coy will get into touch with MAJOR BELLAMY'S force.

13. Two limbers with 100 Shovels & 60 picks & signalling gear will be sent to A Coys H.Q. "A" Coy will take half the tools and send limber on to "B" Coy. H.Q. with remainder, this limber will march with "A" Coy and will return to advanced Bn. HQrs with signal gear. It will collect the tools at the end of the day. Coys are responsible that the correct numbers are handed in.

15. 1 Section T.M.B. will be attached to the Bn. HQ. 1 gun will be at V.12 C.1 and the other at V.12. a.4.

(Sgd) C.W. STOPFORD,
Capt & Adjt.
13 East Lancs Rgt.

14.7.16.

SECRET.   Copies No 12.

Reference 27.S.E.   Operation Order No 2.   14.7.15
Sheet   by Lt. Col. R.I.A. Robinson D.S.O
                     Commanding ...

1. There will be a practice manoeuvring of the WEST HASSINGTON line to morrow.

2. The 13th Bn. E. Lancs. Regt. will parade V7 A 61 at 9 am and will march on new markers on the Bn. parade ground at 6.15 am. ... will be in position on the line at 10 am. Breakfasts at 5 am.

3. Troops will remain in position until further orders are sent by Bde. H.Q.

4. Dress, fighting order, haversack rations will be carried, dinners on return.

5. 2 Lt. WILKS will report to a Bde. Staff Officer at V.11.a.55 and will leave Br. H.Qrs. at 6.30 am.

6. ~~[crossed out lines]~~

7. One N.C.O. and 4 men of B. Coy. already detailed will report at Bde H.Q. P 21 d 8.7.

8. Details left out in accordance with instructions already given — i.e.
   R.Q.M.S   5 Shoemakers   4 C.Q.M.S.
   C.S.M. "D" Coy   4 Tailors   Armr. Sgt.   C.S.M. Turner.
   Master Cook   1 Off. Clerk   4 Pioneers   Cpl. McConnell
   8 Coy. Cooks   1 Post Cpl.   Sgt. Drummer   Stoneman
   1 Sanitary man   1 Servant (O.R.) Drummer Sgt.   Butcher
                                      + assistants
                                      2 Runners   1. Bandsman

9. One limber will march with each Coy. for & from H.Q. with ammunition.

10. The remaining first line transport will carry the B'n. reserve S.A.A. and march with O.C. Coy & B'n. H.Q., dumping S.A.A. there, afterwards returning to V 7 b Central.

11. The Mess cart will go with H.Q. and will return afterwards returning with the first transport.

12. Water if wanted will be drawn from the supply. One water cart will go with B'n. H.Q. to refill two, the other water cart will go with transport.

War Diary.

Operation Order No 3
by Lt. Col R.I.B. Tomson. DSO

1. The Battalion will move on July 19 to relieve the 67th. Inf. Bde. S.W. of Mervis.

2. On our arrival in the allotted area the Bn will come under the orders of the 67th Inf Bde (H.Q. W 25 a 58)

3. The Companies will be paraded in sufficient time to march on markers at 10 am and then march to V 24 via V 20 d 6.2 V 21 d 5.1 : V 23 a 5.8 : V 23 a 1.6.

4. Drill fighting order water bottles to be full & not used in line of march.

5. The Batn will take over Transport lines at V 20 a 5.9.

6. A Guard of 1 Sgt, 1 Cpl & 10 men will be left over tents and bivouacs in the present area (To be detailed by R.S.M.)

7. The Battn Guards at present on Ammunition & water dumps will remain and be rationed by the Unit.

8. The 119th Inf Bde will remain under the 40th Div. for ration & ordnance services, rations for July 19th onwards will be delivered to new transport lines.

9. On the march, a distance of 200 yards will be left between platoons.

10. Personnel of Bde Signalling School & Bde Bombing School will remain behind, they will take over tents vacated by T.M.B.

11. The personnel already detailed to remain behind will remain with new transport lines.

12. After the baggage has been cleared on July 19th the baggage wagons will be returned to No. 2 Coy. 40th Div Train Staple.

13. The camps & transport lines will be left in a clean condition and a certificate to this effect will be obtained from the incoming Unit.

14. Reveille at 5.30 am, breakfast at 7 am. All packs & blankets (in rolls of 10) will be packed & stacked at Q.M. Stores by 6.45 am. Dinner will be served in new camp at V 24 as soon as possible after arrival.

15. Acknowledge.

(Sd) G. W. STOFFORD Capt & adjt
13th East Lancs Regt

July 17/18
Copies to: 1. 119th Inf Bde
2. 2nd in Command
3. O.C. A.B.C. & D Coy

9 Transport Officer
11 Killing Coys
12 & 13 M
14 M.O.

Secret
Maps. 2H
. 27SE
. 36A

No. F3. No 3
NO 11

Operation Orders

by Lt. Col. R.J.B. Johnston DSO.
Comdg 13th East Lancs Regt.
July 1917

1. The Battalion will move on July 17 to relieve the 69th Inf Bde S.W. of Morris.

2. On arrival in the allotted area the Battalion will come under orders of the 87th Inf. Bde (HQ W 25 a 7.0)

3. The Companies will be paraded in sufficient time to march on markers at 10 a.m. & then march to V 24. via V.20d.6.2 V21d.51: V23a.5.8: V23a 1.6

4. Dress. fighting order, water bottles to be full & not used on line of march.

5. The Battalion will take over transport lines at V. 20.a 5.9.

6. A Guard of 1 Sgt. 1 Cpl & 10 men will be left over tents and bivouacs in the present area (To be detailed by R.S.M.

7. The Battalion Guards at present on Ammunition & water dumps will remain & be relieved by this unit.

8. The 119th Inf. Bde will remain under the 40th Div for patrol & ordnance so were, ration for July 19 & onwards will be delivered to new transport lines

9. On the march a distance of 200 yards will be left between platoons.

10. Personnel of Bn. Signalling School and Bde bombing school will remain behind, they will take over tents vacated by TMB.

11. The personnel already detailed to remain behind will remain with new transport lines

(Continued)

Operation Order   No. 9 3.

12. After the baggage has been cleared on July 17th the baggage wagons will be returned to No 2 Co. 40th Divl Train Staple.

13. The Camps & Transport lines will be left in a scrupulously clean condition & a certificate to this effect will be obtained from the incoming unit.

14. Reveille at 5.30 a.m. Breakfast at 6 a.m., all packs & blankets (in rolls of 10) will be packed & placed at R.M. Stores by 6.45 a.m. Dinners will be served in new camp at Vath as soon as possible after arrival.

15. Acknowledge.

(Sd) G.N. STOPFORD Capt. & Adjt.
for Lt. Col. Commdg 13th E. Lancs

Copy No 1 to L.O. HQ Inf Bde
  "   " 2 " 2nd   "
  "   " 3 " H.Q. Command
  "   " 4 " Coys A
  "   " 5 "   "   B
  "   " 6 "   "   C
  "   " 7 "   "   D
  "   " 8 " Transport Officer
  "   " 9 " "
  "   " 10 " "
  "   " 11 " Adjutant
  "   " 12 " Rev. Deary
  "   " 13 " R.S.M.
  "   " 14 " M.O.

SECRET.   OPERATION ORDER No. 4   Copy No.

by Lt. Col. R.H.B. Johnson. D.S.O.

1. The Battalion will relieve the 13th R. Innis. Fus. in the front line sector to-morrow night. Coys. will move independently to their respective Coy. Sectors. No forward movement will begin before 10 P.M.

2. "A" Coy. will take over the right outpost line and "D" Coy. the left outpost. "B" Coy. will take over the right support, "C" Coy. the left support, arrangements to be made between Coys concerned.

3. Companies to move by Platoons, 200 yds. between Platoons.

4. On arriving at the outpost line incoming platoons will lie down and wait until the outgoing platoon has left the post. "A" Coy. will find a post of 1 N.C.O. and 6 men between the supporting platoon and No. 1 Posts and between No. 1 & 2 and between No. 2 & 3. These posts will be withdrawn at daylight.

5. Active patrolling will continue without interruption during relief in the front line. Personnel of the incoming Battn. will accompany patrols of the outgoing Battn.

6. On the withdrawal of the R. Innis. Fus. Steven Coy. Commanders will at once send out patrols working from left to right of Companies.

7. After departure of R. Innis. Fus. the countersign will be TRICK until 6 p.m. on the 23rd.

8. The 12th H. Staffs. Regt. will take over our support & reserve lines. The Support Coys. will arrive at 9.30 p.m. and the Reserve Coys. will arrive at 8.30 p.m.

SECRET.   OPERATION ORDER No 84   Copy No...
(continued)

8. (Contd). As their Platoons come into the trench A & B Coys. will close their Coys. on the right of the trench, D & C on the left the trench. Advance parties will arrive at   to take over trench stores etc.

9. All trenches and billets will be handed over clean. Coy reliefs will be reported to Bn. HQrs.

10. Guides will meet
    "A" Coy at Paradise House at 10.30 pm.
    "D" "   at Batt. HQrs.   at 10.30 pm.
    "B" " } at Batt. HQrs.   at 11.15 pm.
    "C" " /

11. Code word for relief complete "ONIONS"

12. R.S.M. will take over the R. Innis. Fus. Batt. HQrs. and trench stores at 2 pm. leaving an N.C.O. to hand over to the N. STAFFS. REGT.

13. The last named N.C.O. will be responsible that billets and quarters are handed over clean.

14. Lt. MORRIS will parade HQrs at 10 Pm. Coy Commanders will send their mess Kits to Battn. HQrs by 9 Pm.

15. There will be no fires or smoking allowed in the Outposts.

16. The Regt. Aid Post is at E 4 d 5.1.

                              (Sgd) G.W. STOPFORD.
                                    Capt & Adjt.
21.7.18.
                                    13th East Lancs Regt.

SECRET   OPERATION ORDER No 4

by Lt Col G W Stopford 13th East Lancs Regt

21-7-15

1. The Battn will relieve the 13th R. Innis. Fus. Gds. in the front line outpost line tomorrow night. Coys. will march independently to their respective Coy. sectors. No forward movement will begin before 10 P.M.

2. "A" Coy will take over the right No 1 post line, "D" Coy the left outpost. "B" Coy will take over the right support, "C" Coy the left support. Arrangements to be made between Coys. concerned.

3. Coys to move by Platoons ~~300 yds~~ 200 yards between Platoons.

4. On arriving at the outpost line the incoming platoon will deploy in rear and wait until the outgoing platoon has departed the post.
"A" Coy will find a post of 1 NCO & 6 men between the supporting platoon & No 4 Posts, and between No 1 & 2 and between No 2 & 3. These posts will be withdrawn at daylight.

5. Active patrolling will continue without interruption during relief in the front line. Personel of the incoming Battn will accompany patrols of the outgoing Battn.

6. On the withdrawal of the R. Innis Fus. Guards. Coy. commanders will at once send out patrols working from left to right of Coys.

7. After departure of R Innis Fus. the countersign will be TRICK until 6 P.M on the 23rd.

8. The 12 North Staffs Regt will take over our support & reserve lines. Their support Coys. will arrive at 8.30 P.M. As their Platoons come into the trench "A" & "B" Coys will clear their Coys on the right of the trench, "D" & "C" on the left of the trench. Advance parties will arrive at 1. to take over trench stores etc.

9. All trenches & billets will be handed clean. Coy. reliefs will be reported to Battn H.Qrs.

10. Guides will meet:
    "A" Coy at Paradise House at 10.30 P.M.
    "D" Coy at Battn H.Qs. at 10.39 P.M.
    "B" Coy at Battn H.Qs. at 11.15 P.M.
    "C"

11. Code word for relief complete "ONIONS".

12. R.S.M. will take over the R Innis Fus. Battn H.Qs. and trench stores at 2 P.M. leaving an N.C.O to hand over to the N Staffs Regt.

13. The last named N.C.O. will be responsible that billets and quarters are handed over clean.

14. Lt MORRIS will parade H.Qs. at 10 P.M. Coy Commanders will send their Mess Kits to Battn H.Qs by 9 P.M.

15. There will be no fires or smoking allowed in the Outposts.

16. The Regt. Aid post is at E 4 d 5.1.

(Sd) G W STOPFORD
Capt & Adjt
13th East Lancs Regt.

Secret

Warning Notice.

No 5   23.7.18

A. & D Coys & 2 Platoons lent by C Coy will be withdrawn out of the Gas infected area in the event of the projector coming into operation tonight.

Warning will be given by the code word PICKLE. The Companies will be withdrawn North & S. West of the red shading in the accompanying map.

Box respirators should be worn by A & B Coys and the 2 platoons of C. Coy. for 25 minutes from Zero - 10 to Zero plus 15 minutes.

Zero hour will be notified later.

Example PICKLE 2 pm equals projectors will commence at 2 pm. O.C. A & D Coys will re occupy their former positions at Zero + 20 minutes, care being taken to keep on masks if there is any suspicion of Gas.

Watches will be synchronised at 4 pm daily on the telephone.

O.C. B & C Coy. will be on the alert to put on their masks in the event of any suspicion of Gas caused by change of wind.

(Sd) G W Stopford Capt & adj.
13th East Lancs Regt

SECRET   Warning Notice   No 5

1.
A & D Coys will be Platoons but by "C" Coy will withdraw from
Gas infected area in the event of the projector coming into operation to suit
Warning will be given by the Code word PICKLE. The Companies will be
withdrawn N. & S. West of the red in a line from any water.
Box Respirators should be worn by A & D Coys and the 2 Platoons of C
Coy first for 25 minutes from Zero — 10 to Zero plus 15 minutes.
Zero hour will be notified later.
Example: PICKLE 2 P.M. equals projector will commence at 2 P.M
O.C. 'A' & 'D' Coys will re occupy their former positions at Zero plus
20 minutes care being taken to keep on masks if there is any
suspicion of Gas.
Watches will be synchronised at 4 P.M. daily on the telephone.
O/C 'B' & 'C' Coys. will be on the alert to put on their masks
in the event of any suspicion of Gas caused by change of wind.

(Sgd) G.W. STOPFORD
Capt & Adjt

SECRET.   Copy No

OPERATION ORDER. No 6

by Lt. Col. R.I.B. Johnson
D.S.O.

1. The battalion will be relieved by 12th N. STAFFS. Regt. to night.

2. Guides for the front right Coy posts will be sent to "A" Coy H. Qrs at 10.30 p.m.

3. Guides for left front Coy. and for 2 Support Coys will be sent to Batt. H. Qrs at 10.30 p.m.

4. The R.S.M. will hand over all stores and reserve rations to incoming Battn. in the course of the day.

5. During the relief Coy. Commanders of A & D Companies will post out a screen at least 250 yds. in front of their Coys., which will remain there until the relief is complete when it will be relieved by the N. Staffs. Rgt. and join its platoons.

6. Coy. Commanders will see that there is no noise during the relief and that the East Lancs. will man the parapet of the trenches so as to give a free passage to the incoming Battn.

7. Trenches will be scrupulously clean.

8. As soon as Coys are relieved the Coy. Commander will immediately send the code word "HELMET" by runner and signal to Batt. H.Q and march independently back to their old billets at V.24, occupying the same billets there as before

SECRET.　　　　　Operation Order N° 6
(Continued)

8. (Contd). 1 Sergt. per Coy to be sent this afternoon to take over billets from R. Innis. Fus.

9. Distance between platoons 250 yds. Constant touch must be maintained.

10. L/guns and magazines, after relief is complete will be carried from the trenches to ZWITEL VILLA and packed on their limbers there.
N° 1 & 2 will march with the limbers, and will be responsible for the guns.
Limbers will be at ZWITEL VILLA at 12 midnight & Bn's L/gun Sergt will see that they are properly loaded.
Coy. Commanders will be responsible that the full complement of Magazines are returned.

11. Breakfasts will be ready on arrival at V.2.d.

　　　　　　　　　(Sgd) G.W. STOPFORD.
　　　　　　　　　　　　Capt & Adjt.
　　26.7.18　　　　　　13th East Lancs. Regt.

SECRET   OPERATION ORDER No. 6.
                            by Lt Col R.J.B. Johnson D.S.O.

1. The Battn. will be relieved by 12th North Staffs Regt. tonight.
2. Guides for the front right Coy. posts will be sent to "A" Coy. H.Qrs. at 10.30 P.M.
3. Guides for left front Coy & for 2 Support Coys. will be sent to Battn H.Qrs. at 10.30 P.M.
4. The R.S.M. will hand over all stores and reserve rations to incoming Battn. in the course of the day.
5. During the relief Coy Commanders of "A" & "D" Coys. will put out a screen at least 250 yds in front of their Coys. which will remain there until the relief is complete when it will be relieved by the N. Staffs Regt. and join its platoons.
6. Coy Commanders will see that there is no noise during the relief and that the East Lancs will man the parapet of the trenches so as to give a free passage to the incoming Battn.
7. Trenches will be scrupulously clean.
8. As soon as Coys are relieved the Coy Commander will immediately send the code word HELMET by runner-signal to Battn H.Qrs. and march independently back to their old billets at V.24, occupying the same billets as before. 1 Sergt per Coy to be sent this afternoon to take over billets from R.S. minor G.
9. Distance between platoons 250 yds constant touch must be maintained.
10. M Guns & Magazines after relief is complete will be carried from the trenches to LINTEL VILLA and packed in their limbers there. Nos 1 & 2 will march with the limbers and will be responsible for the guns.
   Limbers will be at LINTEL VILLA at 12 midnight and Battn. L/Gun Sergt will see that they are properly loaded. Coy Commanders will be responsible that the full complement of magazines are returned.
11. Breakfasts will be ready on arrival at V.24.

                            (Sgd) G.W. STOPFORD
                                    Capt - Adjt
26-7-11.   13th East Lancs Regt.

SECRET   OPERATION ORDER No 7

by Lt. Col. R.I.B. Tennant
D.S.O.

1. The Battn. will be relieved by the 23rd Cheshire Rgt. to-morrow.

2. Transport will remain in their present camp until further orders.

3. Reveille will be at 5 am to-morrow & breakfast at 6 am.

4. Coy. Commanders will see that all their billets are cleaned and left thoroughly clean by 10 o'clock and ready to be handed over to the 23rd Cheshire Rgt.

5. All working parties will go out fully dressed in fighting order, and after completing their task will be marched by Coy. Commanders to their new camps. Coy. Commanders will be responsible that they do not march off until they have collected all their working parties.

6. Coys. will be marched by Platoons with an interval of 200 yds. between Platoons, care being taken that strict march discipline is enforced.

7. Lewis Gun ammunition will be packed in their boxes in the limbers and will march with their Coys. to new camp but will not be unloaded, and will be put under Coy. Guard.

8. Cookers will be formed at the new camp and dinners will be cooked in them before arrival of troops.

9. Headquarters under Lt. MORRIS will march off at 10.30 am to new camp and will take over H.Q. of 23rd Cheshire Rgt.

(Sgd) G.W. STOPFORD.
Capt. & Adjt.
13th East Lancs Rgt.

29.7.18.

SECRET   OPERATION ORDER No.7
by Lt Col R.J.S. Johnson D.S.O.

1. The Battn. will be relieved by the 23rd Cheshire Regt. tomorrow.

2. Transport will remain in the present camp until further orders.

3. Reveille will be at 5 am tomorrow & breakfast at 6 am.

4. Coy. Commanders will see that all their billets are cleared & left thoroughly clean by 10 o'clock & ready to be handed over to the 23rd Cheshire Regt.

5. All working parties will go out fully dressed in fighting order and after completing their task will be marched by Coy. Commanders to their new camp. Coy. Commanders will be responsible that they do not march off until they have collected all their working parties.

6. Coys. will be marched by Platoons with an interval of 200 yds between platoons care being taken that strict march discipline is enforced.

7. Lewis Gun Ammunition will be packed in tin boxes in the limbers and will march with their Coys. to new camp but will not be unloaded, and will be put under Coy. Guard.

8. Cookers will be found at the new camp and dinners will be cooked in them before arrival of troops.

9. Headquarters under Lt MORRIS will march off at 10.30 am to the new camp and will take over H.Qs of the 23rd Cheshire Regt.

(Sd) G.W. STOPFORD
Capt. & Adjt.
13th Cheshire Regt.

29.7.18

CONFIDENTIAL   W 3

40/119

W.3

"War Diary."

13th East Lancashire Rgt.

August 1918

WARY DIARY or INTELLIGENCE SUMMARY.

Army Form C. 2118.

(Erase heading not required.)

Place	Date	Hour	Summary of Events and Information	Remarks and references to Appendices
V 13 d 11	1/8/16		A and B Coys bathed at RYCK HOOF. Range at STAPLE. C and D Coys at CASTEL. Active to Bn for the day. Coys had Bn inspection before our return.	
"	2/8/16		Range active to the Bn all day. C and A Coys under Capl D coy B Coys under P T & BC Volunteer. Instructors in Company. D and C Coys Bn D/Coys manoeuvres.	
"	3/8/16		Inspection of Bn respirators A and C Coys. B and D Coys manoeuvres. Coys D Coys bathed at HONDEGHEM. Sergt Instructor for Country. Capt the Rev G.E. PICKARD Army (Chaplains dept) taken on strength of Bn. Major S. TABOR assumed command of the Bn on 2/8/16 on departure of Lieut Colonel R.I.B. JOHNSON D.S.O. to take temporary command 119th Inf Bde. (order 3/8/16)	
"	4/8/16		90 men of B.167 inoculated. Bn attended Bde church service at RYCKHOOFE CASTEEL. 4th Anniversary of the outbreak of war. Major the Rev GIBSON senior chaplain from Bn address. Dieu remercier.	
"	5/8/16		S.O.S. Scheme by Bde intelligence officer. Range active to Bn E-1 Bn. Bn went through lachrymatory Chamber at Bde H.Q.	

WAR DIARY
or
INTELLIGENCE SUMMARY.
(Erase heading not required.)

Army Form C. 2118.

Place	Date	Hour	Summary of Events and Information	Remarks and references to Appendices
V.13.d.11	6/8/16		B. Coy inoculated remainder of Bn. Company training. Privates under Platoon Officers.	G.
	7/8/16		In morning Bn training, afternoon recreational training. Bn played 119th Infy Bde H.Q. at football and won by 5 goals to 2. Major Tabor attended a lecture by Genl Plumer on Maps and a Bn demonstration on HONDEGHEM in 36th Divl Theatre. P/O 685.62	G.
—	8/8/16		Bn training. Coy Commanders recommended. W. HAZEBROUCK.	G.
—	9/8/16		Lieut Colonel R.B. Johnson S.O. attended lecture by Genl de la Penouse taken by XVIII Corps School. B Coy. 14.6 B and Paris Pn cleaning training chiefly shooting by sec. boys to mechanical.	G.
			carried on. Training chiefly shooting by sec. boys to machines. The Bn in the attack. Rehearsing competition won by D. Coy.	G.
—	10/8/16		The day was given over to Bn Sports, events were 100 yds dash, 220 yds relay, 1/2 mile race, Bayonet race, Veterans race, 220 yds Officers race, Tug g War and finishing the pole. The weather was fine and Bde band in attendance.	G.

WAR DIARY
or
INTELLIGENCE SUMMARY

Army Form C. 2118

Place	Date	Hour	Summary of Events and Information	Remarks and references to Appendices
V13 d11	10/8/18	9.45 am	Bn held Chinese parade or Bn Football ground.	D.G.
do	10/8/18	9 pm	Capt Buckley F. D/Bn Machine G. despatches date 7-4-18. C.O. went to LUMBRES in afternoon to make arrangements re the 2nd Army School of M.G. ready for the following week. The Bn entrained for LUMBRES arriving at 11 am and went into convoy. Transport proceeded by road arriving at 2.45 pm. Bn H.Q. with all officers billeted in Chateau or the river Aa.	O.O No 12 C.S.
LUMBRES	13/8/18		Review at 5. Frohart at 6. Bns marched to Ren army at 8 am as the range was not available till 1 pm. Coys carried out practising the attack assumes as 12 Loopers being been sent out from 1 to 8 pm Bn Fire practice 1 octoed down M.R.	C.S.
do	14/8/18		Arrangements made for Lewis day. Bn fires of practice of local practice from HYTHE. Loading and appreciation ill local practice of practice of part III fires all rapid and runs loading	C.S.
do	15/8/18		Remaining of practice of practice of practice fired as a whole showed fair measurement in the fire. Coy commanders and C.O. attended a demonstration in the docked and control by Students of 2nd Army Musketry School. Gent Sir H. Plumer KCB sdonn the Stevens 6 and Commanding officers were all attended.	C.S.
do	16/8/18		All Coys carried out Bartle practice by Coys. Lieut Colonel Johnson do actg Brigadier watched the practice carried out which on the whole were fairly good. Company at no the first time the Bn have cleared our Theo practice. Bn returned to see Camp (2mento s evening at V13 d 11 by tarries	C.S.

Army Form C. 2118

WAR DIARY
or
INTELLIGENCE SUMMARY
(Erase heading not required.)

Instructions regarding War Diaries and Intelligence Summaries are contained in F.S. Regs., Part II. and the Staff Manual respectively. Title Pages will be prepared in manuscript.

Place	Date	Hour	Summary of Events and Information	Remarks and references to Appendices
V13 d 11.	17/8/18		The morning was devoted to cleaning up and the bn proceeded and fellny ready for the 119th Inf. Bde Sports which were held in the afternoon at R.Y.C.H. HOOTE C & S TEST U.18. (initial). Bn was lent in the aggregate score for platoon first from 3 pond event the 1/2 mile, 280 yds and 220 yds Officers race.	C.S.
do	18/8/18.	9.45 am.	Bn attended Divine Service in B/n forbear freen. In the afternoon the Bn football team played the 189 Bde R.F.A. and won by 4 goals to 1.	
do	19/8/18		Company training, PM's and boys practicing the attack P.1, rBN. Jas and Elm over there.	
do	20/8/18		119th Bde Field Exey. Bn in defence Lieut Pearce Lt H PEYDON 40th a Reserve (innoven was present	defence Scheme dated 19/8/18. G.O. C.
	21/8/18		Bn moved by route march to MORBECQUE and occupied camp at D2069.6 sheet 36 2 NE (7B local) 2000 arriving at 9 pm	
	22/8/18		Bn left camp at Morbecque at 5 pm arriving at Grand Le Bors at 7.10 pm where they halted till 8.30 pm along to the intense heat. Bn was hurried between the 2nd Bn R. WELCH Fus and occupied the position at the enemy. F20 c 11 - F21 c 14 - F21 a 3.5 CUTLET CORNER B Coy	
	23/8/18		On night: L. Coy on left - A and D in Support, D Coy at LA BIS FARM F13 B and A Coy E.18 d. B.N. H.Q. FAMANAMA F.? B. Reby	
			MOEGHEIN F.10 c.	

Complete by 2. P. Co. Com

WAR DIARY or INTELLIGENCE SUMMARY

Army Form C. 2118

Place	Date	Hour	Summary of Events and Information	Remarks and references to Appendices
VIEUX BERQUIN	23/8/18		On the morning of the 23rd it was decided to move Bn H.Q. to TERN FARM E.17.6 owing to hostile activity from front line and the advance of the night from T.o.1 to a position 600x line F.26.6.5 - F.21.6.2.5 to conform with a forward movement of the 13th R. Innis. Fus. Bn. on our right. During the advance 2nd Lieut SEFTON was killed, the position T.o.1 coming under heavy shell fire. Rations were dumped at Bn H.Q. position T.o.1 (canal)	G
do.	23/8/18		Bn [struck] Lieut Colonel Johnson R.B. DSO assumed command of the 119th Inf. Bde. to enable the Brigadier to proceed on leave. Major S. Tate assumed command of the Bn.	G
do.	24/8/18		Bn. in the same position. Owing to the heavy casualties from shelling in the 2 Infantry Coys. it was decided to keep D Coy. in reserve in moved into position to the 2 front Coys. at F.20.A and F.20.B. This was not carried out by the 10th Commander who was relieved of his command. The movement was however carried out before dawn of the morning of the 25th. Active Battalion was carried out - During the night and at early morning from position located at TIGER FARM F.21.0.9.8 Position from F.21.a.5.6.	G
do.	25/8/18		Bn was relieved on the night 25/26 by the 12th Bn NORTH STAFFS. relief took at by 2.40 a.m. Bn. went into Bde Support in Immediate Position to 12th Bn NORTH STAFFS at E.17.6.2.7. Bn H.Q. Z line E.15.o.1.3.5 - E.9.c.9.5 west of NORTH STAFFS. at Ferme Le Bois E.7.6.9.5	G

Place	Date	Hour	Summary of Events and Information	Remarks and references to Appendices
VIEUX BERQUIN Lieu	26/8/18 27/8/18		Bn in Bois Leppes. The 18th Bn R. Innis Fus. where to attack along the line BECK CORNER F.26.6.10 BISHOPS CORNER at L.3.a.4.0. 2 hour heavy 10.30 am C. Coy then moves forward to deliver an F.2.u at our B. Coy to TERN FARM but Coys & were in position before C.Coy. The R. Innis Fus. found their objective and 2 P.O.S of C. Coy who used to help consolidate the position and 2 P.O.S near C. L. R. Innis Fus. for local attack at Cross A Coy then moved and there placed under C & R. Innis Fus. B. Coy went forward also. Bn H.Q. and D. Coy moved into position E.24.d.2 & Lieut W.M Carter. Liaison officer was mortally wounded by shell fire and Capt & G.P.S. P.18 Stafford was wounded in same place. The Bn relieved the 13th R. Innis Fus. in the new position by A and D Coys in front line & Cosgrove Baud C in support. Bn H.Q. at ROOSTER FARM F.25.a.6.6. Bn had to be removed at once C F.25.a.4.4 owing to heavy and intense shelling from the enemy. from after midnight no more evidence the enemy's move from off the advance before returning to our place at 10 p.m. for which Major Cosgrove M.G. and Capt. Leppes sic. Osgood as also going	Bn in Bois Leppes ⊕
do	27/8/18			⊕
do	28 & 29/8/18			⊕

WAR DIARY or INTELLIGENCE SUMMARY

Army Form C. 2118

Place	Date	Hour	Summary of Events and Information	Remarks and references to Appendices
VIEUX BERQUIN Vicb.	29/7/18 30/7/18	3.40 AM	The Bn was relieved in the line by the 23rd Bn CHESHIRE REGT. relief complete by 3.40 am. Bn marched to Grand Sec Bois where after meal was eaten at 2.30 pm the Bn fell in and marched to a Camp at Le TIRANGLAIS D17 Central. Bn H.Q at SENATOR HOUSE D17 a 6.3.	C.O. No 13
LE TIR ANGLAIS	30/8/16		Bn in Divisional reserve. The day was spent due to movement by 67 [Coys?] [?] and reorganising the 107s. During the 2 tours of the Bn in the VIEUX BERQUIN sector of Came River heavy shell fire and gas attacks principally on the 107s in support, who suffered very heavy casualties. Total casualties for the 2 tours were: Officers killed 2, Officers wounded 45. Other ranks killed 17, Other ranks wounded 4. N.Y.D. Totals for [?] = 33. Total Officers 6 O.R.s 95 G. The trenches held by the Bn was an entirely forward in forward posts held, occupying ways sufficient cover the Garrison at of 4 platoons, it was found it was taken to have the support to keep up thereby avoiding casualties.	

Grey, [Caton?] Major
Cmmdg 1/8 Bn East Lancashire Regt

August 11/18.

Operation Order Nº 12.

1. The Battalion will move tomorrow to LUMBRES for a period of 5 days for Musketry.
2. 32 Lorries will be sent for the use of the Battn. Head of column will be at 27/V24 C 5.7 facing West.
3. Lorries will move off at 9 a.m. embussing to commence at 8.40 a.m.
4. Companies will march to the embussing point independently and will enter their lorries from the north side of the road.
5. Dress fighting order. Blankets will not be taken
6. The first 2 lorries will be used for baggage & S.A.A. the 3rd & 4th for Battn. H.Q.

    Nos. 5 - 11   A. Co.   19 - 25   C. Co.
         12 - 18   B. Co.   26 - 32   D. Co.

7. Transport as detailed will move off at 6.30 A.M.
8. Officers Kit & Mess Gear will be stacked outside Q.M. Stores not later than 5.30 a.m.
9. Officers Spare kits will be handed in to Q.M. Stores tonight.
10. Mens packs, & blankets in bundles of 10 will be sent to Q.M. Stores by 5.30 a.m. tomorrow morning.

(Sd) G.W. STOPFORD

1 C.O.   7 O.C. A Co
2 2nd in Command   8   B
3 Adjt.   9   C
4 T.O.   10   D
5 Q.M.   11 War Diary
6 Sig Officer   12 file
                          13 119th. Inf Bde.

19th East Lancashire Regt.   19/8/18.
Defence Scheme.

Ref. Map. Sh. 27 S.W. Edition 3 B. Local 1/20000.

Information. The Battn is part of a Red Force which has been driven back from W Hazebrouck line. It has reached the line approximately V14 Central V13 Central road past RYCK HOUT CASTEEL U17 a 0.0 Rly in U15 d.c and has been ordered to take up a position on the Staple Hondeghem Ridge. 2 Battns (imaginary) are in O 35 & O 36 in Bde Reserve.

Intention. The Battn will hold the trenches immediately South of the Longue Croisc - le Breard Road at all costs and to dispute all ground in front of it very stubbornly.

Instructions. The line of resistance will run along the trench line from U 5.d 24 to U 5 d 10.0 to U 6 c 71 over Rly crossing down to across the Rly. at U 6 d 61.

A Co. will be on the right and will hold the trench from the right flank inclusive to the communication trench U 12 a 39 exclusive.

B Co. from communication trench at U 5 d 24 up to trench at first Rly. crossing U 6 c 103 exclusive.

C Co. from U 6 c 103 to left flank resting on railway U 6 d 60.

D Co. will be in Battn. reserve in trench just north of Longue Croisc. le Breard Road. with its left flank resting on the Rly at U 6 c 84.

Companies to have 2 platoons in line of resistance with their other 2 platoons in intermediate line and outpost line.

Outposts to be on the Borre Beaque.

Houses in their front will be loopholed & sandbagged for Riflemen & machine guns. The Outposts & intermediate posts will endeavour to fight their battle in front of the line of resistance.

Half a section of T.M. will be at U 5 d 24 & half a section at U 12 b 4.10

Battn H.Q. will be at trench U 5 d 89.

Regtl. Aid Post at house in U 6 a 13.

The line of resistance will be held at all cost. Should any part of the line be penetrated by enemy D Co. will immediately make a counter attack and retake the line. All lightly wounded cases will be attended to by stretcher bearers in the line of resistance & will continue to fight.

Reserve ammunition will be distributed along the line of resistance

Troops will be in position by 9.30. The enemy are wearing steel helmets Red Force caps.

2.

1st line Transport under R.S.M. will be on the road at U 6 a 1.3.

(Sd) G W STOPFORD
Capt & Adjt.

Copies to. A
B
C
D
Bde. H.Q.
T.M.B.
R.S.M.
M.O.
War Diary
file.
Major Tabor.

SECRET.

Operation Order No 7.

By Lt Col. R. B. Johnson D.S.O.
Commdg 13th East Lanc's Regt
Aug 22/1918.

MAP REF 36A NE
1/20,000

1. The Battalion will relieve the 2/4th RWF in the front line of trenches tonight.
   B and C. Coys will be in the front line.
   A " D " " " " support.
   C Coy will take over from A Coy RWF on left
   B " " " " " " B Coy RWF on right
   D " " " " " " D " RWF on left support
   A " " " " " " C " RWF on right support
   Reliefs to be arranged between Coys concerned.

2. 5 Guides per Coy of RWF will be at Fern Farm at 10 o'clock & will guide the platoons into their posts.

3. Touch must be kept up between platoons and between units on right and left flanks.

4. Active patrolling will be maintained immediately the Battn gets into the line.

5. Tomorrows rations and water will be dumped at FERN FARM. and from there carried by Companies to their new line.

6. Battn will parade ready to march off at 5 o'clock. Order of route It. D. B. C. D and A.

7. A distance of 200 yds must be kept between Coys. Lewis gun limbers, one limber for rations and water, 1 cooker, and one pack animal with 2 Boxes SAA. will march in rear of their Coys

"Secret" Operation Order No 7 Continued

8 Company's Officers Mess Boxes must be carried on the limber allotted to their Company

9 Water Bottles must be filled and must be kept for the Trenches. Men are warned that water is extremely scarce and are recommended to economise as much as possible.

10 There will be an hours halt at Petit Sin Bois. Coy Cookers will provide tea for their Coys at this halt.
After the halt Coys will march with platoons intervals of 100 yards.

11 Bn H.Q. will be at Maleghem. advanced H.Q. I.17.d.8.7.
Reg'tl Aid Post will be at a farm just East of Maleghem Farm.

12 Completion of relief will be wired to Battn H.Q. by the code word "Harvest"

Acknowledge

Distribution

Copy No 1. to Bde HQ
    2. CO
    3. Major Tates
    4. Adj
    5. OC A
    6. " B
    7. " C
    8. " D
    9. Lt M Carter
    10. MO
    11. RSM
    12. War Diary
    13. File

(Sd) G.W. STOPFORD.
Capt & Adj
13th East Lancs Regt

SECRET   18 Bn East Lancashire Regt.
                                            No. S.O. 87/1.
              OPERATION ORDER No. 8.

              [illegible subtitle]

1. The Battalion will be relieved in the front sector by the 18th N. Staffordshire Regt. to-night.

2. O.C. troops on to [illegible] cross LA COURONNÉ – VIEUX BERQUIN road before march.

3. 'A' Coy. of the North Staffordshire Regt. will relieve 'A' Coy East Lancashire Regt.
   'B' Coy. will relieve 'B' Coy.
   'C' Coy. will relieve 'C' Coy.
   'D' Coy. will relieve 'D' Coy.

4. Companies will send one guide from each platoon to meet the incoming unit at 9 p.m. at PRESIDENT CROSS.

5. The Battalion will be in Support on completion of Relief. 'C' Coy will occupy trenches in E.17 & the other three Companies will march to SANITAS CORNER, where one guide for each Company will meet them and guide them to respective positions. 'B' Coy will be on the Right, 'A' Coy in centre from N. of road at SANITAS CORNER and 'D' Coy on Left.
   Battalion H.Q. will be at E.7.b.8.6.

6. Previous chain limbers will report at 10.0 p.m. at the dump at TERN FARM.
   1 limber will be used for H.Q. M.G. Section
   1   "   "   "   "   Signalling Gear
   1   "   "   "   "   Empty Petrol tins
   Each Coy. will bring out all empty petrol tins and place them on the dump near Bn. H.Q.

7. Completion of Relief will be notified to Bn. H.Qrs. by wire & runner, code word "CORN".

8. Trench Stores will be handed over & receipts given.

9. ACKNOWLEDGE.

(Signed)
G. M. STOPFORD.
Capt & Major
1st Bn East Lancashire Regt.

ISSUED 1.10 p.m.
25-9-1915.

OPERATION ORDER No. 43

Major [?] Sabor Commanding   Aug-5-1917

1) The Battalion will be relieved in the line tonight by the 25 Bn. Cheshire Regt.

2) 'C' Coy Cheshire Regt. will relieve 'A' Coy. East Lancs.
   'A' Coy.   "   "   "   "   'B' Coy. East Lancs.
   'D' Coy.   "   "   "   "   'C' Coy. East Lancs.
   'B' Coy.   "   "   "   "   'D' Coy. East Lancs.

3) Front Coys. of East Lancs will have 1 guide per post at their Coy. H.Qrs. at 9-p.m. to take reliefs out to their positions.
   'B' Coy East Lancs will provide 4 guides to take 'C' Coy. Cheshires to 'A' Coy. E. Lancs. H.Qrs. and 4 guides to take 'A' Coy. Cheshires to 'B' Coy. E. Lancs H.Qrs.
   'C' Coy. E. Lancs will provide 4 guides to take 'B' Coy. Cheshires to 'D' Coy. E. Lancs. H.Qrs. and 4 guides to take 'D' Coy. Cheshires to 'C' Coy. E. Lancs H.Qrs.

4) 'A' Coy. E. Lancs. will be responsible for the relief of Platoon of 'C' Coy. attached to them.

5) Guides — all guides will report at PRESIDENT CROSS not later than 9-15 p.m.

6) PETROL TINS — Every available petrol tin will be carried out and dumped at PRESIDENT CROSS

7) Lewis Gun Limbers will meet outgoing Companies at MERE FARM.

8) Hot meals will be served as soon as possible after arrival at destination.

9) On completion of relief each Coy will send in CODE-word CHEERFUL to advanced Battalion H.Qrs. and will march their Coys back independently to vicinity of SANITAS CORNER where instructions as to final location will

be given to them:

10. ACKNOWLEDGE:

(Signed)
S. THROR, Major
Commdg 13 Bn East Renvewshire Regt.

Distribution

Copy. 1 - 119 Inf. Bde
2 - 2? Bn Cheshire Regt.
3 - O.C. 'A' Coy.
4 - O.C. 'B' Coy.
5 - O.C. 'C' Coy.
6 - O.C. 'D' Coy.
7 - Commdg Officer
8 - 2nd in Command.
9 - War Diary
10 - File.

WAR DIARY or INTELLIGENCE SUMMARY

Army Form C. 2118

13 E Lanc
Vol 4

W.4

Place	Date	Hour	Summary of Events and Information	Remarks and references to Appendices
LE TIR ANGLAIS	1/9/18		BN at SENATOR HOUSE. Church Parade of all denominations together 10 am.	
	2/9/18		BN marched to PONT WEMEAU F.28.A.40.95. West MERRIS sector I.A. where it bivouacked. Route Steenwerck / Borre / Vieux Berquin, Cutlet Corner.	
PONT WEMEAU	3/9/18		The day was spent in to inspections and examinations under the orders of the 121 Bde.	
STEENWERCK	4/9/18		BN proceeded by route march to Sec16 at A16 C.2.6 near STEENWERCK. Area in very dirty and destroyed condition having been recently vacated by the enemy, it was necessary to keep well under cover as enemy planes were active.	
do	5/9/18		Company Commanders and 2 i/c (Commanders reconnoitred route to the NIEPPE sector. The following officers joined the BN.: Lieut HAWARTH, 2nd Lieuts CALVERT, ADAMSON, H.C. HEMINGWAY and SHEPHEARD J. The BN relieved the 23rd BN CHESHIRE REGT in the Line in the sector Shar. 36 N.W. E.P.9.A and held the position on the N and N.W. of the river LYS running from JESUS FM B.26.D.5.2 northwards along the	
NIEPPE SECTOR	6/9/18		NIEPPE system pt.700 Thorpe points and thence by ten to a point up B.16 at 9.6. The 13th R. INNIS. FUS were on the right and a BN of the EAST YORKS 31st DIV were on the left. The Total frontage held by the BN was approximately 1000 x with the BN holding Strength 369	

WAR DIARY or INTELLIGENCE SUMMARY

Army Form C. 2118.

Place	Date	Hour	Summary of Events and Information	Remarks and references to Appendices
NIEPPE SECTOR	7/9/18		Orders where received that the Bn were to attack and capture the PONT de NIEPPE and establish posts on the W bank of the RIVER LYS. This attack was made in conjunction with a Bn of the East YORKS 31st Div under a barrage ZERO being 10 AM. The Bn formed its objective by 10.30 am and consolidated the posts at B23 a 9.7, B23 a 95.85, B24 c 05.95, B24 a 1.2, B24 a 25.24. During the operation 2 Coys 13th R. Irish Fus were lowered to either the NIEPPE SYSTEM. The 2 Coys attacking A and D were instructed to withdraw during the afternoon being here harrying present Harassing of however the night was employed in MG and rifle artillery on harassing fire also a little for shelling.	O.O. No Return
do.	8/9/18		The day passed off quietly and the Bn was relieved in the line by the North Staffords Lieut Colonel Johnson D.S.O. returned to the Bn from the Base and took over command of the Bn. The BC here in reserve at POSTON IMS at 8.20 at 2.9.	

WAR DIARY
or
INTELLIGENCE SUMMARY.

(Erase heading not required.)

Army Form C. 2118.

Place	Date	Hour	Summary of Events and Information	Remarks and references to Appendices
NIEPPE SECTOR	9/9/18		The Bn moved to NIPPON BEND B.19.B.25.40 and was here in Reserve.	
do	10/9/18		Bn rested in NIPPON BEND	
do	11/9/18		The Bn and 12 R. INNIS FUS changed positions. The Bn moved to LETT FARM and now the INNIS to NIPPON BEND	
do	12/9/18		Bn in reserve at LETT FARM. "C" Coy over a fighting patrol with the object of locating the R.L.Y.C at H.10.40. This they were unable to accomplish as the enemy of the obstructed bridge had been warned away, the men being in fact, they however engaged the enemy with L.G and rifle fire from the river bank, the enemy were also very much on the alert. Lieut EA JAMES had Command of the patrol and 2nd Lieut G.O. CHATTERIGN D.C.M had Charge of the Covering party. There were 11 men. The 1.30 A.M.	
	13/9/18		The Bn were relieved by the 11th Bn CAMERON HIGHLANDERS relief complete 0.0. by 8.20 P.M and moved to Camp at PONT WENEMEAU F.28.A.40.95	

Place	Date	Hour	Summary of Events and Information	Remarks and references to Appendices
PONT WERPEAU	13/9/18		Bn in Brigade Reserve. Total Casualties for the tour in the line, which occurred for the largest part during the attack on PONT DE NIEPPE. Officers one wounded Other Ranks 3 killed 29 wounded 10 missing Total 1 Officer 42 O Ranks.	
"	14/9/18		The morning was given over to cleaning up. In the afternoon a working party consisting of two Companies was furnished for working on roads. The remainder of the Bn were occupied on general work about the Camp.	
"	15/9/18		Church Parade for all denominations together at 9.45 a.m.	
"	16/9/18		Training. Before breakfast Saluting drill without Arms. Morning & afternoon musketry & Platoon Drill. Bathing for all men from 5 to 7 under Coy arrangements.	
"	17/9/18		The Bn furnished working parties for road work under R.E's A & B Coys at 7.45 a.m. C & D Coys at 11.45 a.m. Arms drill for C & D Coys in the morning A & B in the afternoon	

Place	Date	Hour	Summary of Events and Information	Remarks and references to Appendices
PONT WEMEAU	18/9/18		Working parties furnished as on the 17th. The 119th Inf Bde less one Bn were inspected by G.O.C 40th Division at which 6 S.M Lawrence and 33 N.C.O Pte Wilson nr of this Bn were presented with M.M ribands for devotion to duty during tour ending 30-8-18. The Bn transport lines and billets were afterwards inspected by the G.O.C 40th Div.	
	19/9/18		Saluting and Arm drill before breakfast training during morning. Tactical Schemes by Companies. During afternoon recreational training under direction of the Physical Drill Instructor.	
	20/9/18		Training first parade gas drill & saluting. Second parade 2 Coys at tactical schemes 2 Coys general training. All Coys on games during the afternoon.	
	21/9/18		Battalion moved to HAZEBROUCK, Sheet 36 NE/ D-H-c-2-9. in Reserve Bde Area. The move was carried out without particular incident. Good horse billets were procured	O.O.15.

Army Form C. 2118.

WAR DIARY
or
INTELLIGENCE SUMMARY.
(Erase heading not required.)

Instructions regarding War Diaries and Intelligence Summaries are contained in F. S. Regs., Part II. and the Staff Manual respectively. Title pages will be prepared in manuscript.

Place	Date	Hour	Summary of Events and Information	Remarks and references to Appendices
HAZEBROUCK	22/9/18		Check Roll Call, cleaning of billets and whole Bn Bathed.	
"	23/9/18		Bn moved as in O.O. N° 19 to BAILLEUL. D.A.Q.M.G, 40th Div met the train at BAILLEUL with instructions its return by same train to HAZEBROUCK as move was cancelled. Bn occupied the same billets.	O.O. 19.
"	24/9/18. Morning		'A' Coy fired on Miniature Range, remainder of Bn - General Training.	
	Afternoon		Bn Check Roll Call + Muster Parade.	
"	25/9/18		'A' Coy employed salvaging S.A.A. Etc from EAST HAZEBROUCK LINE. G.O.C., 119th Inf Bde inspected C.T.D Coys whilst training. 'B' Coy fired on Miniature Range. M.O. inspected Bn for Skin Diseases. Lt Col Miller, XV Corps Horsemaster inspected Transport and horse gear, Horse Management lecture.	
B 5.d.3.2	26/9/18		Bn moved by train to BAILLEUL. Left BAILLEUL by March route to Clemens at Couriel Farm. Bn relieved 10th East Yorks on left sector of Fide Post outpost line Bn HQ at B.5. D.3.2 (Sheet 36.N.W.2) Relief was completed 2. a.m. Line taken over was an Plaisir-Outpost line Kor Guard in W.R. VARIAVE-	D.O. 20

WAR DIARY
or
INTELLIGENCE SUMMARY

Army Form C. 2118.

Place	Date	Hour	Summary of Events and Information	Remarks and references to Appendices
A.5.D.3.1.	26/4/18		BECORDEL running from C.1.C.15.-60 — B.12.A.65.50. Two Coys held this line with A Coy in support & D Coy in reserve in NIEPPE SYSTEM. 2 /Lt Hennessey was wounded while on Patrol.	
B.5.D.32	27/4/18		Inactive during the day. During the night the Bn took over the whole Bn. Front as Vanguard - extending our line from B.12.A.65.50 — B.17.C.85.90. Liaison posts were established with 31st Division on the left & 121st Division Brigade on Right. All posts on the front were strongly wired. Our patrols were active during the night.	O.O.21
B.S.D.32	28/4/18		Lt.Col. Johnson D.S.O. proceeded on leave to United Kingdom. Major O'Connor 13th Inniskillings took over command of Bn. at 9am. Inactive during the day. All night Stretches were slung across the WARNAVE RIVER & four strong Patrols attempted to cross. The night patrol crossed without opposition to a distance of 150 x yards from own position then act. Patrol then drive back across the WARNAVE. Posts been instructed when practicable to W SIDE of WARNAVE guarding the approach to Pontoon. Two officer patrols then recomt. the River South till Brigade left Bn limits.	

A6943 Wt. W14432/M1160 350,000 12/16 D. D. & L. Forms/C./2118/14.

Army Form C. 2118.

WAR DIARY
or
INTELLIGENCE SUMMARY.
(Erase heading not required.)

Instructions regarding War Diaries and Intelligence Summaries are contained in F. S. Regs., Part II. and the Staff Manual respectively. Title pages will be prepared in manuscript.

Place	Date	Hour	Summary of Events and Information	Remarks and references to Appendices
B.5.D.3.2.	29/9/18		Inactive during the Day. At night orders were received for the Battalion to advance Halfort line Across the R. WARRANG. This was carried out successfully. A new line of posts was established as follows:- C.1.C 15.30 - C.1.C 05.10 - C.7.A 25.85 - C.1.A 40.55 - B.12.B 9.1. - B.12.D 1.6. - B.1R.A 6.9. - B.18.A 85.45 - B.16.B 05.20 - B.18.D 10.95. 2nd Lieut ASHWORTH was wounded.	
B.6.C.55.25.Btfft			Bn.H.Q. moved forward to B.6.C. 55.25. Patrols pushed forward during the Day most opposite of Railway B.12.D 65.40. Lieut BIRKIN was wounded. The patrol were held up by M.G. + Rifle fire + Bombs. Patrols Coys B posts 1502 advanced to C.M.A. 8.6. without strong opposition was met. During the night the leading Vanguard were taken over by the 13th Lancashire Fusiliers. The Relief was completed successfully + the Battalion marched to reserve at TRAS ROPES B. 7.C. 9.8.	

Total Casualties 9 Killed, 54 Wounded, 1 & Obiouring officer J.B. Turner

Major
Comdg. 13th East Lancs Regt.

SECRET

Operation Orders No 13
By Major S. Tabor
Commdg 13th East Lancs Regt

Map Ref
Sheet 36A

Sept 2nd 1918

1. The Battalion will move forward to vicinity of DOULIEU road.
2. The Battn will parade at 9.30 a.m. in fighting kit. Reveille 5 a.m. Breakfast 6.30 a.m.
3. All Packs and blankets to be carried by Coys to wagon lines at 6 a.m. Officers kits & Mess Equipment to be stacked with Coy packs by 7.15 a.m.
4. Bn will rest at VIEUX BERQUIN for 1½ hours for dinner
5. An advance party under 2/Lt Walls consisting of C.Q.M.S. and 2 men per Coy will be ready to move by 7.30. These will be conveyed by lorries.
6. 300 yards distance will be kept between Coys.
7. All water bottles must be filled and kept for emergency. Men are warned that water is extremely scarce in this area and are recommended to economise as much as possible.
8. Lewis Gun Limbers will report at 8.30 a.m. for loads of Coy Guns.
9. Cookers will march with their Coys.
10. Route of March. LE VIR ANGLAIS — TACKLE BRIDGE — SPEARMINT CORNER — SPANDER HOUSE — B 19.6.5. — GLIM FARM — VIEUX BERQUIN.
11. Acknowledge

Copies No 1. C.O.
    " " 2. Bde
    " " 3. 2nd in Command
    " " 4. Adj
    " " 5. O.C. A Coy
    " " 6. O.C. B.
    " " 7. " C.
    " " 8. " D.
    " " 9. T.O.
    " " 10. Q.M.
    " " 11. S.O.
    " " 12. D.L.G.O.
    " " 13. File
    " " 14. War Diary
    " " 15. War Diary

(Sd) T J GOUGH
Capt & Adj.
13th Bn East Lancs Regt

SECRET.   Operation Order No 15

1. The Battalion East Lancs Regt. will relieve the 23rd Middlesex Regt. tonight to-day and take over the Brigade Reserve Trenches in sector [illegible] Subsidiary line on [illegible] B & C Coy. in strongpoint at [illegible]
(R.S.a. centre) in Reserve.

2. B & C Coys will move off once at [illegible] report at Bn. H.Q.

3. Transport will move off at 7 pm [illegible] to new [illegible]
All Tran: port baggage under Major J. V. Lewis.

4. M.G. and three men will remain on guard our present lines until taken over by a Unit of 101st Brigade.
The Guard will then report to the Wagon Lines.

5. The T.O. will detail one mounted orderly to report at Bn. Q.M. by 3 pm for duty with Q.M. & Transport Officer.

6. Ammunition. Two limbers of S.A.A. will be sent [illegible] Bn. H.Q. and remain there. A dump is being [illegible] at new Transport Lines.

7. Water. This is to be carried up in Watercarts filled time to Bn. H.Q.

8. B & C Coys will take tinned rations — A, D Coys and H.Qs have dinners before starting.

9. Relief will be reported by Code Word "BASS"

10. ACKNOWLEDGE.

                                    J H [illegible]
                                    Capt & Adjt.
                                    13th East Lancashire Regt.

Copies No 1 - O.
       "   2. 2nd in command.
       "   3. Adjt.
       "   4. R.Q.M.Qs.
       "   5. O.C. A C.
       "   6. " B C.
       "   7. " C Co.
       "   8. " D C.
       "   9. T.O.
       "   10. Q.M.
       "   11. D.I.Q.O
       "   12. D.I.O.
       "   13. F.R.
       "   14. M.O.
       "   15. War Diary
       "   16.

Orders

O.C. D Coy.   T.J. 57. 7-9-18.

You will attack PONT DE NIEPPE from the northern side of NIEPPE – ARMENTIERE ROAD AAA. Time 10.0 AM.
Objective is WEST BANK of the RIVER LYS. due East of PONT DE NIEPPE AAA.
Company frontage is 200ˣ – keeping the NIEPPE ARMENTIERE ROAD on right flank. AAA. Two sections will be specially detached to deal with any resistance from the houses on East Bank of the River Lys. in B 24 A & C. On gaining Objective posts will be established on the Banks of the River West of Pont de Nieppe with the Platoons in Support AAA.
The 31st. Division is undertaking an operation at same time AAA.
You will endeavour to get in touch with them on completion of operations
The signal for having gained objectives will be three Very lights in quick succession fired in a Northerly direction. AAA
The Barrage opens at 10 am. and will lift 100ˣ every three minutes & will continue until 500ˣ yds beyond the objective – when it will cease.
You will cut wire in front of the NIEPPE SYSTEM by dawn AAA.
2 Grenades per man & 1 bandolier to be carried AAA.
Special attention will be paid to mopping up especially houses in B 24 A 38 and B 18 C 73 AAA.
Liaison posts to be established at Rd Junction B 18 d 17 with 10 E Yorks AAA

FEFE.
2.9 am.

(Sgd) T.J. GOUGH.
Capt. & Adjt.

O.C. A Coy.   T.J. 59   7th 9-18.

You will attack PONT DE NIEPPE from the southern side of NIEPPE-ARMENTIÈRES ROAD AAA Time 10.0 AM. AAA
Objective is WEST bank of river LYS due East of PONT DE NIEPPE AAA.
Company frontage is 300x — keeping the NIEPPE-ARMENTIÈRE ROAD on the left flank AAA
On gaining the objectives posts will be established with the Platoon in Support on the WEST bank of R. LYS. AAA.
You will get in touch with C Coy. on completion of operation AAA.
The signal for having gained the objectives will be three Very lights fired in quick succession in a southerly direction AAA.
The Barrage opens at 10 AM and will lift 100x every three minutes and will continue 500x beyond final objective — when it will cease AAA
You will cut wire in front of NIEPPE SYSTEM before dawn. AAA.
2 Grenades per man & 1 bandolier to be carried AAA.
Special attention will be paid to mopping up AAA.

(Sgd) T.J. GOUGH.
Capt & Adjt.

FFFE.
2.31 AM.

Report on Minor Operations
of Sept 7th. 1918.

Orders from Brigade. B.O.O. N° 35 was received at 12.55 am. 7th inst. Orders as per attached copies were immediately issued to Coys & a conference of Coy. Commanders was held at Battn H.Q.

A & D Coys were detailed to do the attack. A Coy attacking S. of the NIEPPE-ARMENTIERES RD. keeping the road as their left flank; D Coy attacking N. of the NEIPPE-ARMENTIERS RD kept the road as their right flank. Each Coy was given a frontage of 200x with orders for a first objective of W Bank of River LYS.

An Artillery Barrage co operated & put down an extremely good barrage.

At 10 AM. the Barrage started & lifting 100x every 3 minutes searched 2500 yards of ground.

A & D Coys. immediately started over the open & following the barrage very closely were very quickly in the outskirts of PONT-DE-NIEPPE. After this observation became difficult.

D Coy on the left went straight to their objective — keeping their noses up to the barrage the whole way. The attacking force of D. Coy. got to their objective with no casualties, by 10.30 am. The mopping up sections of this Coy suffered a few casualties from M.G. Bullets — but their was very little opposition.

After establishing posts at B23.D99, B24.C0595, B24 A12, B24 A33, B24 A35.40 the party moved N.E. along the river bank with the intention of joining up and getting to into touch with the attacking troops on our left.

They reached a spot B24 a 28 where a party of enemy came out with the intention of surrendering. On approaching them to fetch them in, others of the enemy opened fire from the buildings & the first party ran back into the house. D. Coy. attacking troops then attempted to surround the house.

A Coy established a Post at 23B & 87 on the right & was getting on through the village but met a little more opposition. At 3 P.M. both Companies were on the River bank with posts placed on either side of the road commanding the bridge at B24 c07. Later in the afternoon a party of the enemy from 60-80 strong left the buildings at B24 a 28 & attacked D Coy. who were not more than 30 strong. the Coy. Commander decided to retire fighting as their ammunition was running short and there was a chance of the whole Coy being scuppered, seeing that the Battalion on their left had their attack hung up, & take up position in NIEPPE SYSTEM of trenches. This was safely accomplished & completed by 8.30 p.m.

2

Our Companies inflicted heavy loss on the attacking enemy while fighting in the village on the East side, it is estimated that at least 30 of the enemy were killed as when the Coys were holding the posts they had favourable opportunity to strike at close quarters range. An attempt was also made at the same time by the enemy to capture the post established by the right Lt Coy. in this they did not succeed and they retired to their original jumping off position, fighting their way back through the village.

The initial success of the attack was due to the rapidity with which the Coys followed up the barrage to their final objective.

It cannot be too clearly brought out that it is absolultely necessary in an operation of this nature that the mopping up parties should be considerably stronger than the front line.

The total strength of the 2 Coys engaged did not exceed 105.

All Officers & men showed great courage under exceptionally difficult conditions.

SECRET

RELIEF ORDER.   8/9-18.

1. 18th Bn East Lancs will be relieved by the 12th N. Staff Regt. tonight 8th inst.

2. D Coy. N Staffs will relieve A & D Coy EAST LANCS
   C "   C Coy
   A "   N   B Coy

3. OCs A & D Coys will each send two guides to meet D Coy N Staffs at the CRUCIFIX B21.B3180. Guides to be at arranged spot at 7.30 pm.

4. OC B & C Coys will each send sufficient guides to meet C & A Coys N Staffs at the CROSS ROADS at ORVILLE JUNCTION. Guide to be at arranged spot at 7.30 pm.

5. All ammunition & any stores to be handed over to Coys. taking over & receipts obtained.

6. Bn. HQrs. will be at B19 B3 4

7. A Coys. EAST LANCS billets are at HUTTED Camp B20 A0590
   B   B20 A4040
   C   B19 B45
   D   B20 A0590
   Bn. Hd.s. Coy.   B19 B15 30

8. A limber will meet A & D Coys at CRUCIFIX B21 B3180 for L Gunners & Magazines. A limber will meet B & C Coys at ORVILLE JUNCTION.

9. Hot meals will be ready on arrival at Billets.

10. Great attention must be paid to lighting fires in vicinity of Billets. No movement to take place by day. All men must be kept under cover. On completion of relief of A & D Coys "I" R.I. mans Fus will report to their own unit.

11. Code word on completion of relief "CHIPS".

12. Acknowledge.

            (Sgt. T.J. GOUGH
               Capt & Adjt.

SECRET   Operation Order No. 17
         By Lt Col R B Johnson D.S.O.
            Commanding 13 Bn East Kent Regt
                                    Sept 12 1917

1. The 19 Inf Bde will be relieved by the 120 Inf Bde as advanced guard of the 40 Divn on the night of 13/14 Sept.

2. The 13 Bn East Kent Regt will be relieved by the 11 Camerons on night of 13/14 Sept.

3. Two Guides will be sent by each Coy and by Bn H.Q Coy to meet the 11 Camerons at RAILWAY CROSSING B.25 a 8.7 at 7.30pm.

4. A B C & D Coys 13 E Kents will be relieved by the corresponding Companies of the 11 Camerons and will march off independently when their Coy relief is complete.

5. Reser H.Q O.M. and Transport will move off independently.

6. All ammunition and bombs will be handed over to the incoming Coys and receipts obtained. These to be rendered to this office by noon 14 inst.

7. New billeting area will be at PONT WEMEAU with Bn H.Q. at same farm as previously.

8. An advance party of all Coy. QMS under 2/Lt A Peterkin will proceed to PONT WEMEAU by 4-30pm. This party to include a Pioneer for H.Q.

9. All cookers will proceed to new camp directly after teas have been issued and will have hot tea ready for the men on arrival (at about 9.30pm)

10. One limber will report to B Coy at 6-45 pm and load up Lewis Guns and magazines and then proceed to A Coy and pick up theirs
   One limber will report to D Coy at 6-45pm and load up Lewis Guns and magazines and then proceed to C Coy.
   2 Limbers and Mess Cart & M.O's Maltese Cart to report at these H Qrs at 6.45pm

11. Accomodation for Q.M Stores and transport lines will be taken over from 11th Camerons

12. ACKNOWLEDGE

(Sg) T. J. GOUGH
Capt & Adjt
13 Bn East Lancs Regt.

DISTRIBUTION

Copy No. 1   C O
      2   2nd in Command
      3   Adjt
      4   119 Inf Bde
      5   O C A Coy
      6   " B
      7   " C
      8   " D
      9   T.O
     10   Q M
     11   M O
     12   S O
     13   A/ADJT
     14   11 Camerons
     15   File

Orders

Map Ref 36NW
                                                                Dec 4/1918

1. The Battalion will move [illegible] [illegible] to the
   vicinity of A.M.C.
2. The Battalion will parade at [illegible] in fighting
   order.
3. Limbers for Lewis Guns and Ammunition [illegible]
   loaded at 2.15 p.m. and march with their
   Companies.
4. All Trans will be taken forward.
5. The usual march discipline will be observed.
   be 300 yds between Companies.
6. All water bottles to be filled and kept for
   emergency. Men are warned that water is
   extremely scarce in the area and are recommended
   to economise as much as possible.
7. The three cookers already sent will march with
   the Battalion. Tea will be prepared on the
   march ready for issue on arrival.
8. March parade:
      PONT WEMEAU – LE VERRIER – WINK COTTAGE
      LE GRAND BEAUMART – A.16.a.
9. Acknowledge.

Copies No 1. C.O
   "   " 2 2nd in Command   Capt & Adj.
   "   " 3 Adjt
   "   " 4 Bn HQ   13th Bn East Lancs Regt.
   "   " 5 O.C. 'A' Coy
   "   " 6   " B
   "   " 7   " C
   "   " 8   " D
   "   " 9 T.O
   "   " 10 Q.M.
   "   " 11 B.C.O.
   "   " 12 B.I.O.
   "   " 13 T.M.
   "   " 14 M.O.
   "   " 15 WAR DIARY
   "   " 16

Operation Orders. No. 2.   20-9-18.

MAJOR H. WILCOX.
Comdg. 13th. E. Lancs. Regt.

1. The 117th. Inf. Bde. will relieve the 121st. Inf. Bde. in Reserve Bde. Area on 21st. Sept. 1918.
2. The 13th. East Lancs Regt. will relieve the 23rd. Lancs Fusiliers.
3. Bn. H.Q. will be at D.H.Q.
4. The Battalion will entrain at BAILLEUL at 2.20 p.m. 21st.
5. An Advanced party under Lt. Wells, consisting of 1 C.Q.M.S. per Company, 1 Sigr. 1 H.Q. N.C.O. & 1 Officers Stores, will parade with cycles at 9.30 A.M. and proceed to new billets and take over from 23rd. Bn. Lan. Fus. Bde.
   The C.Q.M.S. & H.Q. N.C.O will meet the Battalion at HAZEBROUCK STATION to guide the Battalion to their new Billets.
6. Coys will render entraining state by 8.30 A.M. 21st. to H.Qs.
7. Two lorries will report at these H.Qs. at 12 noon for all packs & blankets. All Packs & blankets (rolled in bundles of 10) will be stacked at Corner by main road by 10.30 a.m.
8. An advanced loading party will parade at these H.Qs. at 10.30 A.M. consisting of 1 N.C.O & 8 men (to be detailed by B Coy) and proceed to BAILLEUL STATION for unloading the lorries & loading on to the train.
9. Coys will parade ready to march off at noon in the following order H.Q. A, B, C, D. with an interval of 200 yds. between Coys.
10. All Lewis Gun Limbers to be packed & ready to move by 10.30 A.M.
11. A loading party consisting of all the Tailors & Bootmakers will load the packs & blankets on to the lorries at this end at 12 noon.
12. All Coys will have dinners punctually at 11.15 A.M. Teas will be ready for the Battalion on arrival at HAZEBROUCK.
13. All H.Q. Mess kit to be ready for loading at 11.45 A.M.
14. All Officers kit, & Coy. Mess boxes to be dumped at Battn. H.Qs. by 10.30 a.m. together with H.Q. Stationery boxes & Coy Stationery boxes.
15. No Officers Chargers will be taken to BAILLEUL.
16. Two G.S. Waggons will report at HAZEBROUCK STATION & meet Battalion to convey Blankets to Billets. All packs will be carried.
17. ACKNOWLEDGE:

1. 117th. Inf. Bde.   12. T.L.O.
2. C.O.   13. Enquiry
3. 2nd. in command   14. O.C.
4. O.C. A.Q.
5. " B.
6. " C.
7. " D.
8. Q.M.
9. T.O.
10.
11.

F. J. Gough.
Capt. & Adjt.
13th. Bn. East Lancs Regt.

SECRET.

MAP REF. 36 N.W.

Copy No.

Operation Order No. 20.

by LT. COL. JOHNSON. D.S.O.
Cmdg. 13th East Lancs. Regt.

1. The 119th Infy Bde is relieving the 92nd Bde on night 26/27th.
2. The 13th East Lancs. Regt. is relieving the Left Half Battn. 10th East YORKS.
3. B & C. Coys will be in Outpost Line and relieve the Left Coy of the 10th EAST YORKS. A. Coy in support & D. Coy in Main Line of Resistance in NIEPPE SYSTEM.
4. The Battalion frontage will be from Railway B.12. A.b.b. to ROAD C.1. B.12. (Railway & Road inclusive).
5. B. Coy front will be from B.12. A.b.b – C.1. C.0.5. (Railway inclusive). A Liaison Post with the 13th INNISKILLING FUS. of 1 N.C.O. & 3 men to be established at B.12. A.80.45.
6. C. Coy front will be from C.1. C.0.5. to C.1. B.1.2. (Road inclusive). A Liaison Post with 31st Division of 1 N.C.O. 3 men is to be established at C.1. B.1.3.
7. A Coy will be in support to D & C. in B.5.D. with H.Q.s approx B.5.D.97. D Coy will be in Reserve in NIEPPE SYSTEM in B.4. A.B.T.G. with Coy. HQs at B.4. C.9.9. and will link up with the 13th INNISKILLING FUS. on Right and 31st Division on Left.
8. Sufficient Guides will meet the Coys at B.10. A.8.9. at 8 pm.
9. The Battalion will move from present billets at 7.45 A.M. and proceed to HAZEBROUCK STATION to entrain for BAILLEUL.
10. Men will carry packs (slung) to station. All blankets to be rolled in 10s and dumped in main street (MERVILLE ROAD) by 5.30 A.M.
11. Officers kits to be packed and dumped in main street not later than 6. A.M.
12. Breakfasts for the Battalion at 6 A.M. 2 Cookers will proceed at 6 A.M. to COMMET CAMP, & have dinners ready by 12 o'clock.
13. Officers surplus mess kit will be carried on transport & dumped at wagon lines at A.16. B.0.5. This will be stacked on main road beside kits.
14. A loading party consisting of the Regtl. Tailors will load the blankets & proceed to the station for unloading, and remain there until arrival of the Battn.
15. Coys will render entraining states by 7 A.M.
16. Relief complete will be notified by Code word "COCKLES". - by wire and runner. Map locations of Coy. H.Qs. will also be sent.
17. ACKNOWLEDGE.

(Signed) J. J. Gough.
Captn & Adjt.
13th East Lancs Regmt.

WAR DIARY

13th E. LANCASHIRE REGT

MONTH OF OCTOBER

WAR DIARY
or
INTELLIGENCE SUMMARY.
(Erase heading not required.)

Place	Date	Hour	Summary of Events and Information	Remarks and references to Appendices
NIEPPE AREA ARMENTIERS	1/10/18		B^n relieved by 13th B^n R INNIS FUS and moved back to area B7d (Sheet 36NW) RABOT WNW of NIEPPE. The day was spent over to cleaning up and of reorganization. B^n H.Q at B7d.9.8	
	2/10/18		B^n emp^ld on Coy training range at B7d 9.61 PT and B^F hand-ling of arms and LG inspection. Inspection by L.O and M O S inspection	
	3/10/18		B^n Training. Runs Relay in the morning at 1.30pm B^n moved forward to the NIEPPE SYSTEM B^n H.Q at B10 b 2.5. Coys in area B10.6 and B11 c	
	4/10/18		B^n moved at 2.30 a.m to take up position in trenches t the 12th B^n N STAFFS over the River LYS EAST of HOUPLINES NE of ARMENTIERS. A Coy in area C.22a B/o/ C.22 c C.16y C.16a D/oy C.22c. B^n H.Q at C.22 C.20.65 (Sheet 36NW) 2nd Lieut SHARPLES took over (command) of A Coy 1 (casualty) in B Coy	

Army Form C. 2118.

WAR DIARY
or
INTELLIGENCE SUMMARY.
(Erase heading not required.)

Instructions regarding War Diaries and Intelligence Summaries are contained in F.S. Regs., Part II. and the Staff Manual respectively. Title pages will be prepared in manuscript.

Place	Date	Hour	Summary of Events and Information	Remarks and references to Appendices
ARMENTIERS	3/10/16		B.N. Still in billets. The B.N. was relieved by the 15th B.N. K.O.Y.L.I. and proceeded to LE BIZET C 13 c.l. Capt. EVANS returned and resumed command of B Coy	
NIPPON	6/10/16		B.N. moved with Bde into support Z B 19 a Sher 36 N.W.	
BEND			B.N. H.Q. B 19 a 1.3	
"	7/10/16		Day given over to cleaning up and inspections. Lieut Colonel R.J. ANDREWS D.S.O. M.C. late C.O. 17th S.B.N. The WELSH REGT (1st GLAMORGAN) joined the B.N. and assumed command.	
"	8/10/16		The B.N. has better all. Kleanis and hear coals were promulgated	
"	9/10/16		B.N. Training under Coy arrangements.	
"	10/10/16		P.M. Training. Lectures: Lewis Gunners etc. and the above officers	
"	11/10/16		Coy Training. E Coy sent to trench	
"	12/10/16		B.N. relieved by 23rd CHESHIRES and moved into Divisional Reserve at MUTTON FARM A 11 a 3.3. Arrangements for	

WAR DIARY
or
INTELLIGENCE SUMMARY.
(Erase heading not required.)

Army Form C. 2118.

Place	Date	Hour	Summary of Events and Information	Remarks and references to Appendices
	13/9/18		Bn. moved to billets accommodation with B & H Bns situated at A.10.a.70.95. Church parade and route march in the morning to room	P.
A.10.a.70.95	14/9/18		Bn training GOC and other Senior Bn. Infantry & in Battle Drill and advance by the G.O.C Report on Battalion. Bn. marched passed in column of route. Pres about forming carried out G.O.C Interview all officers & N.C.O. Parol	
"	15/9/18		A. Coy on range, remainder of Bn. DIEB: Open. Breve and bayonet stations, Bn. offer from transfer on range. and lecture to our offices on F.C.P Post. 14 Bng. Gene Carbin Bng. BDO at STEENWERCK.	P.
"	16/9/18		Bn. training in the attack L.G. on range by Coys in morning and B.	P. 1
	17/9/18		Bn. moved by route march to GOSPEL VILLA H.72	P. 00
	18/9/18		Bn. moves by route march to J.1.A sheet 36.a 7000 via ERQUINGHEM-LYS-ARMENTIÈRES-HOUPLINES	00
	19/9/18		Bn. moved into old enemy camp in J.1.B and worked on the P.	P.

WAR DIARY
or
INTELLIGENCE SUMMARY.
(Erase heading not required.)

Army Form C. 2118.

Place	Date	Hour	Summary of Events and Information	Remarks and references to Appendices
J.1.B.	19/9/18		Railway to LILLE in the sector between PERENCHIES and STANDRE	G
J.1.B	20/9/18		work on firing day on railway, the Bn marched and retired 5 kilometres of Rly.	G
"	21/9/18		Bn training L.G. & rifle p.m's and toys in the attack	G
"	22/9/18		Training Bn in the attack L.G on range, in morning practice with smoke and rifle grenades in a strong points in afternoon all ranks who had not fired grenades were instructed and all ranks where two hundred have to fire and leave the L.G.	G
	23/9/18		Bn honored with the Bele for Promotion of decorations to recipients by Lieut. Genl Sir H PEYTON KCB DSO. SERGT WRIGHT, CORPL LEVEN and Pte SHANNON received the M.M.	G

WAR DIARY or INTELLIGENCE SUMMARY

Army Form C. 2118.

Place	Date	Hour	Summary of Events and Information	Remarks and references to Appendices
BONDUES	24/10/18		BDE. moved by route march to BONDUES. The BN does as advanced guard to the BDE and an attack was carried out against The Town. This has done as an exercise and the BN was held up near the 19th Q Gunns and 12th N Staff passed through when the BDE moved to their fields. BN was billeted in good barns with BN H.Q. in the CHATEAU VERT BOIS 6.12.d – F.7.c – F.13.a Sheet 36 et 7000	O.O.
BONDUES	25/10/18		BN olivier under The C.O. L.C.s on range in afternoon. BN marched with Bde who were lent lorry to WATTRELOS and broke off to go to CROIX where The BN was specially employed on the railway lines under the Canadian Railway Corps.	G
do	27/10/18		Was on the previous day. The Commanding Officers and Officers attended a thanksgiving service at the French Church at CROIX at the special request of the Curé on the liberation of the Town from the Germans by the 1st D.E.N.N.	G

A6945 Wt. W14422/M1160 350,000 12/16 D. D. & L. Forms/C/2118/14.

WAR DIARY
or
INTELLIGENCE SUMMARY
(Erase heading not required.)

Army Form C. 2118.

Place	Date	Hour	Summary of Events and Information	Remarks and references to Appendices
Lys	27/10/18		was sent, a picked party of N.C.O.S and men. From the B.N. reinforcements the Division who had relieved the Town on that Service. The C.O. and officers not employed picked party attacked Divine Service or the English Church. The Tanks and Divisional Commander were also present. The Sufferings and hardships which the French People today of 28 tanks had for through clothing. The 4 years and 3 days that the enemy were in Lorbin despite desperate times drove the inhabitants had no means for men 2 years they were insulted and most of their homes were stripped of every one thing & more even the stone roads and were from the mostly were taken away	G
WATTRELOS	28/10/18		The B.N. moved by route march to WATTRELOS where on arrival the Bde and was billeted in houses in the evening a Concert was held	G

WAR DIARY
or
INTELLIGENCE SUMMARY.
(Erase heading not required.)

Army Form C. 2118.

Place	Date	Hour	Summary of Events and Information	Remarks and references to Appendices
WATTRELOS	29/10/18		Bn. training all Coys practised the attack, each Coy alternating with a Pn under the Company Officers. P.T., B.F. and Box Rest also taken. Specialists under their respective Commanders. A delayed action mine went off near the railway station in the afternoon killing 3 officers and 3 other Ranks of the 13th R. Berks Regt. The 13th having sent 3 Coys with Lewis & Lewis guns & fires from the roof. A Pn of ours have before the G.O.C. in the an of Coys No. 1, 2 and 3. 6. Remainder of Bn. practice Pn and Coy in the attack. In afternoon ceremonial forming and salute Coy for Roll Call. Drums which have been reformed by the Adjutant played for the first time.	G
do	30/10/18			G
do	31/10/18 →		Bn. training demonstration by C.O. of new formation of the Pn in the attack carried out later by all Coys, formation practice ceremonial found Mounting made by B.S.M.	G

A.F.Manning Lt. Col.
Commdg. 13th Bn. R. Berkshire Regt.

SECRET.   OPERATION ORDERS. 21
                    by Major E. O'CONNOR. 3-10-18
                         Cmdg. 13th East Lancs Regt.

1. The Battn. will move forward today to positions in the
   NIEPPE SYSTEM.

2. Each Coy. will send parties consisting of Coy. Commander, 1 NCO,
   + 1 man per platoon as soon as possible to reconnoitre new
   position. They will remain.

3. The Battn will parade ready to march off head of column to be
   at Battn H.Q. facing N.E. at 13.45.

4. Order of march   Battn H.Q.
                     A Coy
                     B "
                     C "
                     D "

5. Destination. NIEPPE SYSTEM about B10B – B11C. Battn H.Q. will be
   at B10c25.

6. ROUTE. Main Road to NIEPPE to B16 A32 thence N.E. to position.
   Coys. Guides will meet Coys. at B10D70

7. Packs, Blankets, Bivouac Sheets, extra S.A.A., Grenades etc. to be
   stacked by Coys. at Battn HQ. 12.00.

8. Transport will return as soon as new sites are fixed up
   to these H.Q. and convey kits, bivouac sheets, ammunition
   etc. forward.

9. Acknowledge.

                              (Sgd) T. J. GOUGH.
                                   Capt + Adjt.
Distribution.   No.   13th East Lancs Regt.
    119 Infy. Bde.   6
    C.O.   2
    O.C. A Coy.   3
     "   B "   4
     "   C "   5
     "   D "   6
    M.O.   7
    War Diary.   8
                        9
    File.   10

SECRET.   OPERATION ORDER   No 21   by Lt/A
                                E Coy 5th Northamptons.

Ref Map
Sheet 36-27 1/40000.

1. The Battalion will attack enemy positions north
   28th inst at WATTRELOS area.

2. Battalion will form up with head of column at Rendez-
   at 10.55 hrs

3. Order of March A Coy, B Coy, C Coy, D Coy.

4. First line transport will march with Bn
   at rear of ... Companies will march
   with 10 yards interval between Coys.

5. The strictest march discipline will be
   observed on the march.

6. All Company Commanders will be mounted.
7. Watches will be synchronised at 0900 hrs.
8. The men fighting order under the scouts
   will ...... will be at 0910 hrs.

9. Dress fighting order. Steel helmets will
   be worn. No pack need be carried.

10. KITS BAGGAGE
    All packs must be stacked in Coys
    outside their Company Lines, labelled
    rolled in 10s labelled by 0900 hrs
                                                E.T.O.

PAGE 2

11. Officers Valises & Mess Kit must be packed & stacked by 0930 hrs.

12. Marching Out States must be at Orderly Room by 0930 hrs.

13. Marching In States by one hour after arrival.

14. All billets must be left in a clean & sanitary condition & certificates rendered to this effect must be at Orderly Room by 1000 hrs.

15. Reveille 0630 hrs Breakfast 0730 hrs. Dinners on arrival at new billets.

16. ACKNOWLEDGE

(SD) T. J. GOUGH
Capt & Adjt.
13th Bn East Lancashire Regt

DISTRIBUTION
Copy No 1 O i/c Force
         Commanding Officer
         2nd in Command
         Adjutant
         H.Q. A
             B
             C
             D
         R.S.M
         T.O & QM
         M.O
         S.O
         DIARY
         "
         15. File

SECRET   OPERATION ORDER   No 21

1. [illegible]
   [illegible]

2. [illegible] WATTHERS [illegible]

   Battalion will [illegible] head of column
   at 10.25 [illegible]

3. Order of March [illegible]

4. [illegible] transport [illegible]
   [illegible]

5. [illegible]

6. All Company Commanders [illegible]

7. [illegible]

8. [illegible]

9. [illegible] fighting order — [illegible]
   [illegible]

10. KIT & BAGGAGE
    All [illegible]
    [illegible]

                                    P.T.O.

11. Officers Valises & Mess Kit. nr at H.Qrs + packed by 0930 hrs

12. Marching Out States must be at Orderly Room by 0930 hrs.

13. Marching In States by one hour after arrival

14. All billets must be left in a clean & sanitary condition & a certificate to this effect must be at Orderly Room by 1000 hrs.

15. Reveille 0630 hrs Breakfast 0730 hrs. Dinners on arrival at new billets.

16. ACKNOWLEDGE

(Sd) T. J. GOUGH
Capt & Adjt.
13th Bn East Lancashire Regt

DISTRIBUTION
Copy No 1 H.Q. of Bde
      "   Commanding Officer
      "   2 i/c
      "   Adjutant
      "   A Coy
      "   B   "
      "   C   "
      "   D   "
      "   R.S.M
      "   T + M.M
      "   M.O
      "   S.O
      "   DIARY
                    15. File

SECRET   OPERATION ORDERS 2?
                    by Major E O'CONNOR 3-10-17
                        Cmdg. 13th East Lancs Rgt.

1. The Battn. will move forward today to positions in the
   NIEPPE SYSTEM.

2. Each Coy. will send parties consisting of Coy Commander, 1 NCO,
   + 1 man per platoon as soon as possible to reconnoitre new
   position. They will remain.

3. The Battn will parade ready to march off head of column to be
   at Battn H Q. facing N E. at 1345.

4. Order of march   Battn H Q
                     A Coy
                     B "
                     C "
                     D "

5. Destination NIEPPE SYSTEM about B10B - B11C. Battn H.Q. will be
   at B10 C 25.

6. ROUTE Main Road to NIEPPE to B16 A 32 thence N E to position.
   Coy. Guides will meet Coys. at B10 D 70

7. Packs, Blankets, Bivouac Sheets, extra SAA, Grenades etc. to be
   stacked by Coys. at Battn HQ s 1200.

8. Transport will return as soon as new sites are fixed up
   to these HQ and convey kits bivouac sheets ammunition
   etc. forward

9. Acknowledge

                                    (Sgd) T. J. GOUGH.
Distribution   No.   Capt & Adjt.
                                       13th East Lancs Rgt
    119 Infy Bde.   6
    C O   2
    O C   A Coy   3
          B   4
          C   5
          D   6
          M O   7
    War Diary   8
                           9
    File   10

13th East Lancs Regt
OPERATION ORDER No. 21
6-10-18

Sh. 36 N W
1/20000

Reveille 11.00
Breakfasts 12.00
Dinners — on arrival.

MOVE The Battn. will move to huts in B19 and B20 this afternoon. Coys will march off independently at 10 minutes interval. HQ Coy (under Lt Adamson) leading at 2 PM followed by A B C & D Coys.

ROUTE C 7 C 9.3 – PONT NIEPPE B 23.6.05 – B 28.6.2.7 –

Guides will meet Battn at B21 a 7.3

All billets will be left clean.

Acknowledge

04 00

(Sgd) H.L. WELLS
2 Lt
A.A.

13th East Lancs Rgt.
OPERATION ORDER No. 21
6-10-18.

Sh. 36 N.W.
1/20000.
Reveille 11.00
Breakfasts 12.00
Dinners — on arrival.

MOVE. The Battn. will move to huts in B19 and B20 this afternoon. Coys. will march off independently at 10 minutes interval. H.Q. Coy. (under Lt Adamson) leading at 2 P.M followed by A. B. C & D Coys.

ROUTE C 7 C 9.3 — PONT NIEPPE B 23-6-0.5 — B 28-6-2-7 —

Guides will meet Battn at B 21 a 7.3

All billets will be left clean.

Acknowledge

04.00.

(Sgd) H.L. WELLS
2 Lt.
A.A.

6a

SECRET

OPERATION ORDERS. No 22.
by Lt. Col. R.J. ANDREWS, DSO. MC.,
CMDG 13TH BN EAST LANCS REGT, 11-10-18.

SHEET 36 N
1/20000.

1. The Battn will move into Reserve Area to A11.a.33 tomorrow 12th inst and will be relieved in Support Area by 23rd Cheshire Regt.

2. The Battn. will pass N & S Grid line through B-19-a O.O between 14.45 and 15.15.

3. Coys will move off independently at 200 yards interval, complete with L.G. limbers and Cookers, in following order: HQ. B.C A-D Coys. at 14.45. Strict March Discipline will be observed.

4. DRESS. — Battle Order.

5. An Advance Party, consisting of C.Q.M.S's and 4 men per Coy. will move off under 2nd Lt. A. LEE. at O9.OO hours carrying haversack rations. Coys. will as far as possible, occupy the same billets as previously occupied.

6. PACKS & BLANKETS will be stacked by Coys. by 0845 near road of respective Camps.
OFFICERS VALISES 11.00 Mess Equipment 13.30.

7. Reveille 06.00 Breakfast 07.30 Dinners 12.00 Tea 16.30.

8. Transport Lines & Q.M Stores will not move.

9. Marching Out State will be rendered by 12.00
Marching In States soon after arrival.

10. A Certificate will be rendered that all Billets and vicinity are in thoroughly clean and sanitary condition, and open latrines filled in.

11. All canvas with exception of Battn property will be left standing.

12. Recreation Room will be handed over complete.

13. Completion of move will be notified by code word "JOAN".

14. Acknowledge.

(Sgd) H.L. WELLS.
2Lt.
a/Adjutant.
13th Bn East Lancs Regt.

SECRET OPERATION ORDER No 22 (COPY) No 11

Sheet [illegible] 2nd Lieut. R.J. Andrews, etc
1/20,000 Comdg. 13th Bn. East [Surrey Regt]

1. The Battn will move into Reserve Area by [illegible] on the 12th inst and will be relieved in Support [illegible] by 23rd Cheshire Regt.

2. The Battn will pass N of S [illegible] line through [illegible] between 14.45 and 15.15.

3. Companies will move off independently at 200 yards interval, complete with L.G. [limbers] and cover, in following order: "A", B, C and D Companies at 14.45. Strict March Discipline will be observed.

4. DRESS — Battle Order.

5. An advance party, consisting of C.Q.M.S.'s and 12 men per Company will move off under 2/Lt. S. Lee at 09.00, carrying haversack rations.
Companies will, as far as possible, occupy the same billets as previously occupied.

6. PACKS and BLANKETS will be stacked by Companies by 08.45 near road of respective camps.
Officers' Valises, 11.00 Mess Equipment 13.30

7. Reveille 06.00, Breakfast 07.30, Dinners 12.00 Tea 16.30

8. Transport Lines and Q.M's Stores will not move.

9. Marching Out States to be rendered by 12.30
Marching In States soon after arrival

10. A Certificate will be rendered that all Billets and vicinity are in thoroughly clean and sanitary condition, and open latrines filled in.

11. All canvas with exception of Battn property will be left standing

12. Recreation Room will be handed over complete

13. Completion of move will be notified by code word "JOAN"

14. Acknowledge.

(Signed) H. Wells
2/Lt.
a/adjutant
13th Bn East Surrey

Filing

DISTRIBUTION LIST

No 1 — 119 Inf. Bde
" 2 — C.O.
" 3 — 2nd in Command
" 4 — Adj.
" 5 — OC "A" Company
" 6 — "   "B"   "
" 7 — "   "C"   "
" 8 — "   "D"   "
" 9 — Transport Officer
" 10 — Q.M.
" 11 — Filing
" 12 — War Diary
" 13 — "   "
" 14 — "   "
" 15 — Asst Adj
" 16 — R. Eto,

Mark "Secret"

SECRET OPERATION ORDER   12.
SHEET 36 NW
1/20,000

1. On 17th October 1918 116th Inf Brigade
    will move to camps vacated by
    120th Inf Brigade in the NEUF-BERQUIN
    Area and will remain in Divl Reserve
    The Battn will move to H.3.a.5.1
2. An advance party under 2/Lt Adamson
    consisting of C.Q.M.S's & one man per Coy
    and Regtal Sergeant will leave at
    0700 tomorrow morning sharp.
3. All surplus kits will be dumped at
    once at Battn H.Q. and will be moved
    to Divl Surplus Kit Dump STEENWERK
4. O.C. "C" Coy will detail a guard of
    1 N.C.O. & 3 men (crocks) to remain to
    guard over Present Camp with 2 days rations
5. Battn H.Q. will close at present location
    at 0930 and open at new H.Q. at H.3.a.5.1
    at 0930
6. Transport & QMS Stores will move to
    H.3.a.5.1
7. Cookers & L.G. Limbers will march with
    Companies
8. The Battn will move independantly
    in the following order. H.Q.(under 2/Lt Seymour)
    A.B.D & C usual intervals & strict march
    discipline to be observed.
9. Coys will move off at 0720.
10. Acknowledge.

                    (Signed) Reynolds
                              2/Lt
                              Adjt
                              16th Bn Cheshire Regt

Distribution List.

No 1. to 119 Duty Bde
" 2 "   C.O.
" 3 "   2nd in command
" 4 "   Adjutant
" 5 "   O/c "A" Coy
" 6 "   " "B" "
" 7 "   " "C" "
" 8 "   " "D" "
" 9 "   Transport Officer
" 10 "   Quarter Master
" 11 "   Filing
" 12 "   War Diary
" 13 "   "
" 14 "
" 15 "   Asst. Adjutant
" 16 "   R.S.M.
" 17 "   Signal Officer
" 18 "   Medical Officer
" 19 "   L.G. Officer

15

1. On [ ] October 1918 the [ ] Inf Brigade will relieve in camps vacated by [ ] Inf Brigade in the NORTH ESQUIMALT Area and will remain in billets until the Battn will move to H.Q. a.51

2. An advance party under 2/Lt [ ] consisting of C.Q.M.S's & one man per Coy and Signal Sergeant will leave at [ ] tomorrow morning, [ ]

3. [ ] surplus kits will be dumped at Battn H.Q. and will be moved [ ] Surplus Kit Store STEENWERK

4. O.C. "B" Coy will detail a guard of (N.C.O. & [ ] men (cooks?)) to remain in charge over present Camp D. with 2 days rations

5. Battn H.Q. will close at present location at 0930 and open at new H.Q. at H.3.a.51 at 0930

6. Transport & Q.M's Stores will move to H.Q. a.51

7. Cookers & L.D. Limbers will march with Companies

8. The Battn will move independently in the following order:- H.Q. (under 2/Lt Seymour) A, B, D & C normal intervals & strict march discipline to be observed.

9. Moves will move off at 0720

10. Acknowledge

(Signed) A.H. Wells
2/Lt

8

Distribution List

No 1. to 119 Infty Bde
" 2 " C.O.
" 3 " 2nd in command
" 4 " Adjutant
" 5 " O/C "A" Coy
" 6 " O/C "B" "
" 7 " O/C "C" "
" 8 " O/C "D" "
" 9 " Transport Officer
" 10 " Quarter Master
" 11 " Filing
" 12 " War Diary
" 13 "
" 14 "
" 15 " Asst. Adjutant
" 16 " R. S. M.
" 17 " Signal Officer
" 18 " Medical O
" 19 " L. G. O.

Operation Order No. 11
by Lieut A J Andrews D.S.O M.C.
Comdg 15th Can Rens Bn
17-10-18

1) The Bde is moving tomorrow 18th October 1918 to BIZET to HOUPLINES and NOUVEL HOUPLINES

2) The Battn will move to billets in C 27 B 2.0 approx at 08.00 hrs.

3) All tents, blankets etc will be struck and dumped together with blankets, packs and surplus kit at Bn HQ by 07.00.

4) The advance party will parade at 07.00 at Bn HQ as already detailed under 15/ O daws m.

5) Transport will be Brigaded under Lt. C.S. Hare to 17th C Inf Bde. at C.27 - c. 0.6

6) One ration per Man will be carried in H.S. rifle TC - 2 biscuits, Rations and tins as per 5 day list.

7) Coys A C D A B and D will detail one man each and O.C. B Coy will detail 4 officers' Mess to guard rear Battn Dump. They will be rationed under Units arrangements until further orders.

8) Bde HQ will open at TOCQUET PARMENTIER at 10.10 hours 18/10/18 and open at C 27. a. 40 at some hour.

9) Location of Bn HQ will be notified on arrival.

10) Daily Battle Order (Particular attention will be paid to the filling of water bottles, Jam Rations and Ammunition.)

11) Battn will be ready to move at 08.10 Order of March - # A B C D. Cookers and Lewis Gun Limbers will march with Company.

12) Marching out State to be rendered by 07.00

13) Acknowledge.

DISTRIBUTION LIST.

No 1.   to   11th Inf. Bde.
" 2   "   C.O.
" 3   "   2nd in Command
" 4   "   Adjutant
" 5   "   O.C. A Coy.
" 6   "   O.C. B "
" 7   "   O.C. C "
" 8   "   O.C. D "
" 9   "   Transport Officer
" 10   "   "
" 11   "   Filing
" 12   "   War Diary
" 13   "   do
" 14   "   do
" 15   "   Regt. Adjutant
" 16   "   Q.M.
" 17   "   Signal Officer
" 18   "   Medical Officer
" 19   "   Lewis Gun Officer

DISTRIBUTION LIST

1 to Hq Inf. Bde.
2 " C.O.
3 " 2 i/c
4 " Adjutant
5 " O.C. A Coy.
6 " O.C. B "
7 " O.C. C "
8 " O.C. D "
9 " Transport Offr.
10 " Q.M.
11 " File
12 " War Diary
13 " do
14 " do
15 " Asst. Adjutant
16 " [illegible]
17 " Signal Offr.
18 " Medical Offr.
19 " Lewis Gun Offr.

Secret   ...ation Order No. 25   Copy No. 12.
                          by Lt. Col. R.J. Andrews D.S.O, M.C.
                          Commdg. 13th East. Lancs. Regt
                                              10 October 1918

Short.

    Reveille 06:00   Breakfast ...

1) The Battn. ... ...

2) The Battn. will parade at 06:30 - column of Route facing
   east, in following order - ... ... Head of
   column at jof track at T.6 - 3.4 n (just east of present
   camp). Distance to new billets — 6.00 yards. Cookers will
   march with Coys.

3) Transport will move independently. Transport for ... ...
   will report at 06:00

4) Dress — Battle Order.

5) The camp will be left in a thoroughly clean and
   sanitary condition. Certificates to this effect will
   be rendered to Battn. H.Q. on arrival.

6) The new camp will be cleaned up and
   sanitation will receive immediate attention.

7) Provost Sgt, police and prisoners will remain
   in present camp until 07:00 and will ensure
   that the camp is ... ...

8) Officers H.Q. and Mess equipment will be carried
   in Coy. Mess ... Limbers.

                              (Signed) W.L. Wells.
                                        Lt. & Adjt.
                                    13th Battn. East Lancs. Regt.

Distribution List

No 1 to 119 Inf. Bde
" 2 - C.O
" 3 - 2nd in Command
" 4 - Adjutant
" 5 - OC "A" Coy
" 6 - " "B" "
" 7 - " "C" "
" 8 - " "D" "
" 9 - Transport Officer
" 10 - Quarter Master
" 11 - Filing
" 12 - War Diary
" 13 - do
" 14 - do
" 15 - Asst. Adjutant
" 16 - R.S.M.
" 17 - Signal Officer
" 18 - Medical Officer
" 19 - Lewis Gun Officer

Distribution List

No 1 to 119 Inf. Bde
" 2 " C.O.
" 3 " 2nd in Command
" 4 " Adjutant
" 5 " O.C. 'A' Coy
" 6 "   " 'B' "
" 7 "   " 'C' "
" 8 "   " 'D' "
" 9 " Transport Officer
" 10 " Quarter Master
" 11 " Filing
" 12 " War Diary
" 13 "   do
" 14 "   do
" 15 " Asst. Adjutant
" 16 " R.S.M.
" 17 " Signal Officer
" 18 " Musket Officer
" 19 " Lewis Gun Officer

Secret.

Operation Order No 26
by
Lt. Col. R. J. Andrews. DSO. M.C.
23=10=18.

Copy No 4

Sheet. 36 1/40,000.

1) The Brigade will march tomorrow to the BONDUES area.

2) An advance guard scheme will be carried out in connection with the move.

3) Brigade will march as under.

Advanced Guard. (Commander Lt. Col. R. J. Andrews. DSO., M.C.)

13th East Lancs. Regt.

Main Body
Bde H.Q.	09.00 hours.
T.M.B.	09.02 do
13 R. Innis. Fus.	09.03 do
12 N. Staffs.	09.18 do

Starting Point
Road junction J.1.D.44.

Route Perenches — LA CROIX — FORT DU VERT GALANT — WAMBRECHIES — E.27.C.06. — E.27.A.92 — E.21. — E.22. — BONDUES.

4) A halt will be made about mid-day for dinners.

5) Distances on the march will be
between Coys 100 yards.
" unit and transport 100 yards.
" Battalions 500 yards.

6) All first line transport will march with the battalion except baggage wagons which will march in rear of MAIN BODY.

7) A BILLITING party under 2/Lt. Adamson consisting of Coy. 2. M.S's (& H.Q.) at 07.45 hrs, & will meet the staff captain at BONDUES Church at 10.00 h tomorrow.

8) Dress. FIGHTING ORDER — STEEL HELMETS to be WORN. no sandbag or parcels will be carried.

9) All watches will be synchronised at 07.00 hours.

10) REAR GUARD. A rear guard under 2/Lt PEMBERTON consisting of 2 men per a Coy and one L/Cpl from 'A' Coy will report to adjutant at 06.00 hours

11) **Kits and Blankets**. All packs will be stacked by coys in front of chateau by 06:20 hours. Also blankets rolled in bundles of 10 and labelled. Officers kits by 06:45 at same place.

12) Marching out states to be rendered by to the adjutant by 07:15 hours. Marching in by one hour after arrival.

13) BILLETS will be left in a thoroughly clean & sanitary condition. Certificates will be rendered to this effect before marching off.

14) REVEILLE   05:45 hours
    BREAKFAST   06:30 hours

SCHEME AS IN PARA 11

15) The Battn will march as under:
    Advance Guard (Commdr. Lt. E. James)   "D" Company
    VAN GUARD   (" 2/Lt P. MACTAVISH)   "A"   "
    MAIN BODY   (" Major S. TABOR)   Battn H.Q. "B" "C" Companies on road.

16) The Battn will parade in the above order at 07:30 hours, head of column at Chateau gates.

17) SCHEME The enemy are retiring from the West bank of the BASSE DEULE RIV. Corps Cyclists are keeping in touch with them.

18) The 40th Div has been ordered to pursue vigorously.

19) The 119th Infantry Brigade group will march tomorrow (24. Oct. 1918) as under:-
    ADV. GUARD (Commdr Lt Col A.J Andrews DSO MC)
    1 Battery R.F.A.. (imaginary).
    1 Section R.E. (do)
    1 Section M.G Coy (do)
    13th EAST LANCS. REGT.
    1 Section FIELD AMB (imaginary)
    MAIN BODY
        Bde H.Q.s
        T.M.B.
        13th R. INNIS. FUS.
        12th N. Staffs Regt.
        M.G Coy (less one section)
        Field Coy RE (do)
        Bgde RFA (less one Battery) } (imaginary)
        Field AMB (less one section)
        Coy train

20) 121st Inf Bde (imaginary) are advancing on route LA MITRE — LAMBERSART — ST ANDRE — MARCQ-EN-BAROEUIL.
    120th Inf Bde (imaginary) are advancing on route:-
    QUESNOY — SUR — DEULE — LE CHIEN — LA VIGN

21) Reports to head of main body. Lt Col A.J Andrews DSO MC

22) Connecting files will take up positions as the Battn moves off
23) One G on the bugle is the signal to halt upon which all ranks will fall out without closing up
24) Strict march discipline will be observed.
25) Acknowledge.

2/4
act. adj.
1st East Lancs. Regt.

DISTRIBUTION

Copy No (1)   1/4 Inf Bde
     (2)   O.C
     (3)   2nd i/c
     (4)   Adjutant
     (5)   O.C A Coy
     (6)   do B do
     (7)   do C do
     (8)   do D do
     (9)   T.O. & 2 M
     (10)   M.O & L.G.O.
     (11)   War Diary
     (12)   do
     (13)   FILE
     (14)   R.S.M.

Adjt

SECRET

OPERATION ORDERS   No 26
BY
SHEET 86   Lt Col R J ANDREWS DSO MC
1/40000   23/10/18

1. THE Brigade will march tomorrow to the BONDUES area

2. An advance guard scheme will be carried in connection with the move.

3. Brigade will march as under
   ADVANCE GUARD (Commander Lt Col R J ANDREWS
                                      DSO MC
   13th East Lancashire Regiment

   MAIN BODY
   Brigade Headquarters   0900 hours
   T. M. B.   0902   "
   13th R Innis Fus   0903   "
   12th North Staffs   0918   "

   STARTING POINT
   Road junction J1.d.44
   ROUTE   PERENCHIES — Lt CROIX — FORT — DU —
   VERT — GALANT — WAMBRECHIES — E2Y.C.0.6 —
   E2Y a 9 2 — E 21 — E 22 — BONDUES

4. A halt will be made about mid-day for dinners

5. Distances on the march will be:
   Between Companies 100 yards
      "   Unit transport 100 yards
      "   Battalions   500   "

6. All first line transport will march with the Battalions except baggage wagons which will march in rear of MAIN BODY

7. A billeting party under 2/Lt ADAMSON consisting of Company & Headquarters Q.M.S will parade at 09.45 & will meet the Staff Captain at BONDUES Church at 1000 hours tomorrow
                                            PTO

8. DRESS Fighting order will the rifles
to be worn. No sandbags or parcels will
be carried.

9. All watches will be synchronised at 0700

10. REAR GUARD
A rear guard under 2/Lt Pemberton
consisting of 2 men per Company +
1 Lance Corporal from A Company will
report to Adjutant at 0600 hours

11. Kits & Blankets
All kits will be checked by
Companies in front of Chateau by 0620 hrs
also Blankets rolled in bundles of ten & labelled.
Officers' kits by 0645 at same place

12. M.T. States to be rendered to the
Adjutant by 0715.
M.T. charges in one charge after arrival

13. Billets will be left in a thoroughly clean &
sanitary condition & a certificate rendered to
this effect before marching off

14. ROUTE

15. The Battalion will march in the following order:-
ADVANCE GUARD (Commander Lt E.A. JAMES)
VAN GUARD ("   2/Lt PEMBERTON)
A. Company
MAIN BODY ("   MAJ. S. TABOR
BATT. HQRS. B. C. Companies
The Battalion will parade in the above
order

17. SCHEME

18. The 40th Div has been ordered to pursue vigorously.

19. The 119th Infantry Brigade group will march tomorrow Oct 24th as under.

    ADV GUARD (Commander Lt Col R.T. ANDREWS DSO MC)
    1 Battery R.F.A (imaginary)
    1 Section RE (")
    1 "   MG Coy (")
    13th East Lancs Regt
    1 Section Field Amb (")

    MAIN BODY
    Brigade HQ
    T.M.B
    13th R. Innis Fus.
    12th N. Staffords Reg.
    Machine Gun Coy (Less one section)
    Field Coy R.E. (" " ") } (imaginary)
    Brigade R.F.A (" " Batt)
    Field Amb   (" " Section)
    Company train

20. 121st Infantry Brigade (imaginary) are advancing on route LA MITERIE — LAMBERSART — St ANDRE — MARCQ ENBARŒUL. 120 Infantry Brigade are advancing on route QUESNOY SUR DEULE — LE CHIEN — LA VIGNE.

21. Reports to head of main body to Lt Col R.T. ANDREWS DSO MC

22. Connecting files will take up positions as the Battalion moves off.

23. One "G" on bugle will be the signal to halt upon which all ranks will fall out without closing up.

24. Strict march discipline will be observed

25. ACKNOWLEDGE

                                    [signature]
                                    2/Lt actg/adjt
                                    13th Bn East Lancashire Regt

DISTRIBUTION

Copy No 1 — 119 Inf Bde
2 — C.O.
3 — 2nd i/c
4 — adjutant
5 — OC A
6 — OC B
7 — OC C
8 — OC D
9 — TO + QM
10 — MO + LEO
11 — WAR DIARY
12 — WAR DIARY
13 — FILE
14 — R.S.M

Secret.   Operation Orders.   No 27.   Copy No 4

by Lt Col R. J Andrews D.S.O. M.C.
Commanding 13th East Lancs Regt
October 25/1918

Sheet 36   1/40,000

1) The Bde will move to WATTRELOS area tomorrow October 26th, the Bn to area of CROIX breaking off from main body at F.14.a.5.2.
2) Starting point & roads at F.14.a.5.7.
3) Route MOUVAIX — ROUBAIX.
4) The Battalion will parade in column of route. Head of Column to be at Bn H Qrs facing S.E. at 08.40 hours.
5) Order of March H.Q. A. B. C & D. Coys.
6) The strictest march discipline must be observed on the march. Intervals between Companies 10 yards, between Battalions 25 yards. Transport 100 yards between each 12 vehicles.
7) All Commanders will be mounted.
8) Watches will be synchronised at Bn H Qr at 08.00 hours.
9) The same billeting party as detailed in Operation Orders 26 will report with bicycles to 2/Lt H.E. Adamson at 07.45 at Bn H Q. ~~and meet Staff Captain at Aix 33 at 09.00 hrs for billeting~~
10) <u>Dress</u> Fighting order — Steel Helmets will be worn during the whole march. No Sandbags or parcels to be carried.
11) All Iron rations and mugs must be carried inside the Haversack.
12) Transport arrangements will be notified later.
13) <u>Kits and baggage</u> All packs will be stacked by Coys in front of Coy Orderly Rooms by 06.45 hrs. Blankets rolled in 10's and labelled. Officers Men Kit and Valises to be dumped at same place by 07.30 hours.
14) <u>Marching Out States</u> to be at Bn H.Q. by 07.30 hrs.
15) <u>Marching in States</u>   do   by 1 hour after arrival.
16) A Lorry will report for blankets and packs during the morning.
17) The R.Q.M.S. will detail one guide for the above lorry to be at Bde H.Q. at 09.00 hours. The Regtl Shoemakers & Tailors will be left behind as a loading party for this lorry.
18) <u>Billets</u> All Billets must be left in a clean and sanitary condition. Certificate to this effect to be rendered to this Office. P.T.O.

O.O. 27 (continued)
SECRET   copy no _____

    before marching off.
19) Reveille 06.00 hrs
    Breakfast 07 00 –
    Dinner on arrival at new billeting area

20) Acknowledge

                  (signed) T.J. GOUGH
                          Capt & Adj
              13th Bn. East Lancashire Regiment

Distribution
1) 119 Inf Bde
2) O C
3) 2 I/c
4) Adj
5) O/c A Coy
6) — B —
7) — C —
8) — D —
9) R.S.M
10) T.O. & Q.M.
11) M.O
12) ~~Kentucky~~ S.O
13) WarDian
14) —
15) File
16) Asst. Adj.

Secret.   Copy No 4

Operation Orders No 27
by Lt Col. T. A. Andrews D.S.O. M.C
Map Ref.   Comdg 13th Bn. East Lancashire
Sheet 36.   Regt.
1/40,000   Oct. 25th /18

1. The Brigade will move to WATTNES area
   tomorrow October 26th. The Bn to area of CROIX breaking off from main
                                   Body at F.29.a.5.2
2. Starting Point X Roads at F.14.a.5.7
3. Route MAUVAIX - KRIBAIX.
4. The Battalion will parade in column of route
   head of column to be at Batt. S.P facing S.E
   at 0840 hours
5. Order of march Head Quarters ABCD
   companies
6. The strictest march discipline must be observed
   on the march. Intervals between companies
   10 yards between Battalions 25 yards.
   Transport 100 yards between each Bn.
   Vehicles.
7. All Company Commanders will be mounted
8. Watches will be synchronised at Batt. S.P
   at 0800 hours.
9. The same billeting party as detailed in
   O.O. 26 will report with bicycles at
   ~~the N.C assumed at 0700 at Batt. H.Q +~~
   ~~will~~ ~~staff billets at A.a.3 at 0900~~
   ~~hours for billeting~~
10. ~~Dress~~ Fighting order, steel helmets will
    be worn during whole march no
    sandbags or parcels to be carried.

SECRET O.O. 27 continued

11. All iron rations and emgcy rats must be carried inside the haversacks

12. Transport arrangements will be notified later

13. **Kits** and **blankets**. All packs will be stacked by companies in front of Company Orderly Rooms by 0645. Blankets rolled in twos and counted. Officers mess kit + valises to be dumped at same place by 0730 hours.

14. **Marching Out** States to be at Batt H.Qs by 0730 hours.

15. **Marching In** States to be at Batt H.Q by one hour after arrival.

16. A Lorry will report for blankets + packs during the morning.

17. The R.Q.M.S will detail one guide for the above lorry to be at Brigade H.Qs at 0900 hours. The Regimental shoemakers + tailors will be left behind as a loading party for the lorry.

18. All billets must be left in a clean sanitary condition. Certificates to this effect will be rendered to this office before marching off.

19. Reveille 0600, Breakfast 0700, Dinner on arrival in new billeting area.

770

SECRET. O.O. 27 continued.

2. Acknowledge

(SD) V. J. Govett
Capt & A.
8th Bn. Ess. [illegible]

Distribution.

Copy No	
1	Brigade
2	Officers Cmdg
3	2nd in Command
4	Adjutant
5	OC A Coy
6	" B "
7	" C "
8	" D "
9	R. Sgo
10	TO & QM
11	M.O
12	S.O.
13	War Diary
14	"
15	File
16	Asst Adjt

Confidential

WAR DIARY

of

13ᵀᴴ Bₙ East Lancashire Regiment.

Month of November 1918.

WAR DIARY
or
INTELLIGENCE SUMMARY.

(Erase heading not required.)

Army Form C.2118.

Place	Date	Hour	Summary of Events and Information	Remarks and references to Appendices
LEERS NORD	1/11/18	2 pm	Bn moved by Route March to LEERS-NORD in H.2.b Sheet 37. Billets occupied owing to Bn and details of 2 other Bns being also billeted here.	Q.
do	2/11/18		The morning was free. Sun ran & Lofcorn Wireless Training in the afternoon. A competition was held for the best singing Pl. in the Bn. This was carried out before the Divisional Commander and won by the 13th R Bns. This was a pierced Pl. from Bn.H.Q. commanded by the Bn Signal Officer. Wreath carried after death of demonstration after Parade lecture by the Nazi Staffers who were hateful 2nd The Village was viewed with H.Y. casualties among civilians.	Q. Q.
do	3/11/18		Church Parade all denominations after Parade lecture by Divisional Adj. and 1st Lieut B.G Seymour on Venereal diseases. Coy (Demonstration) Adj. and 2nd In Command visited H.Q and saw area by 23rd Lancashire Fusiliers at ESTAIMBOURG and PECQ to make arrangements for relief on the following day	Q.

WAR DIARY or INTELLIGENCE SUMMARY

Army Form C. 2118.

Place	Date	Hour	Summary of Events and Information	Remarks and references to Appendices
PECQ	4/11/18		The Bn relieves the 23rd Bn Lancashire Fus in the line at PECQ. Their 3 Coy ran from 16.05 to C.25.6.0.5. A Coy on right with posts over the ESCAUT at Le RIVAGE I.6.8.3. B Coy on the left. D Coy in immediate support. D Coy in reserve. Bn H.Q. at Chateau in ESTAIMBOURG B.6.a.1.1. Commanding Officer reconnoitred line and reafforted posts. Ou Le RIVAGE	
do	5/11/18		The only means of crossing the ESCAUT on our front was by means of a single plank footbridge at the main denolished bridge in PECQ I.2.a.5.2. and enemy t heavy rain and flood. This was often torn adrift from being over the line we continually held in touch with the enemy by day and night patrols along Le RIVAGE and by recon. Parties alike both day and night. The patrols being well led, location and strength of enemy were ascertained with a minimum of casualties. I N.C.O. Killed and 3 men wounded.	

WAR DIARY or INTELLIGENCE SUMMARY

Army Form C. 2118.

(Erase heading not required.)

Instructions regarding War Diaries and Intelligence Summaries are contained in F. S. Regs., Part II. and the Staff Manual respectively. Title pages will be prepared in manuscript.

Place	Date	Hour	Summary of Events and Information	Remarks and references to Appendices
Pozy Etaples	9/4/17	11:15 am	be attempted to push on over the ECAUT the enemy having been reported to have retired. At 11.40 am 2nd Lieut. CHADDERTON D.C.M. C. Coy went two platoons in advance to cover the crossing at 1.8 at 85.10 (Pontoon bridge) and rush in force would expect on the right (5.9.2nd Div) He crossed the river below the point by a foot bridge and worked NORTH along EAST side of the river and scanned sunk road west the SOMERSET k.l. at 1.8 at 55.40. At this time the S.M k.l. had fallen back and was crossing the EAST being of the river west the extra Zon of L.P.N which was reputed to be in the village BEAUCOURT with the aid of Artillery. Another attack was made. A hostile M.G was located at 1860r which was replacing our men. 2nd Lieut Chadderton received orders from O.C 11th Som L.I. to deal with the M.G which he succesfuly did covering it to retire in a N.E direction. His position was then heavily Trench Mortared by enemy hostility. There were no only had one man wounded.	

WAR DIARY
or
INTELLIGENCE SUMMARY.
(Erase heading not required.)

Army Form C. 2118.

Place	Date	Hour	Summary of Events and Information	Remarks and references to Appendices
PEC Q Qualino			On the centre 1 Pln of A Coy under 2nd Lieut McLELLAN was detailed to advance along Le RIVAGE from PEC Q Qualino to X roads at I.3.a.6.3 to test enemy strength and locate M.G. position. The road being very open to the Pln proceeded along S side of embankment and on reaching the craters at I.2.G.6.3 was met with a shower of bombs and rifle fire. 2nd Lieut McLellan was slightly wounded and a light armoured car made its appearance. A second attempt was made to cross the crater. They came under exceptionally heavy M.G. and rifle fire from the front and both flanks and T.M.s from close E. Attempts to dig in on N bank were forced impossible on account of heavy M.C. fire. At 13.45 2 Plns of A/164 under 2nd Lieut Macdonald after a good shoot by our Artillery on the craters and houses at X roads in I.3.a attacked across with 1 Pln on each side of company. They immediately came under heavy T.M. and M.G. fire which was very accurate many from	

WAR DIARY or INTELLIGENCE SUMMARY

Army Form C. 2118.

Place	Date	Hour	Summary of Events and Information	Remarks and references to Appendices
P.E.C.Q Junction	6/4/16		Many Germans, 2 L.G.S being knocked out, were however thrown out and fired grenades and Stokes bombs into the Crater. One enemies counter attack was made to occupy the Crater M.G. position. The M.G. and T.M. Co. to keep many of our men being killed and suffering from shell shock. Many killed and 2 wounded, we were however forced on leaving their men back. Two listening posts were established on the E side of main Crater. On this date the Bn. had men considerably and also knew depth in the Bn. fort bridge. A patrol however along the road to 126.1.3 and met with the enemy in C. fin. from both flanks. During the day P.E.O & Co. heavily shelled by H.E. and Lachrymatory shells cause casualties but men in preparation to the intensive bombardment. D. Coy relieved A. Coy in the night.	
	7/4/16		A. and 1/2 of one of the B. Coy were accompanied by 03.05 Am from men being from 18.6.a.5.0. 6.26.a.5.0. 1000 yards frontage. Between 04.30 and 08.00 Bn H.Q and A. Coy were	

WAR DIARY
or
INTELLIGENCE SUMMARY.

Army Form C. 2118.

Place	Date	Hour	Summary of Events and Information	Remarks and references to Appendices
			Heavily shelled by all calibres mostly 8 inch at least 300 shells being sent over. This was several gas casualties in A Coy. These have been several direct hits on B' H.Q. and gas masks had to be worn for 2 hours.	
	8/4/18		At 11.30 to 13.10 a daylight patrol of one N.C.O. & 2 men was sent out to test the enemy strength. SERGT SPENCE 1 Co. in Command of 8 O.R. with S.H. & Scouts attached advanced along the RIVAGE from P.6.c & further. This patrol advanced along S side of road to a distance of about 450 yds and came under harassing fire when about 300 yds forward and on the heighted movement M.G. fire from direction of ATTEMPT was made to flank on E.W. & fire was too heavy. The patrol having accomplished its object withdrew The C.O. crawl over the snow and has nearly betrayed. Careful examinations were necessary to per lack and no casualties have suffered. The position of enemy M.G.S having been	

WAR DIARY
or
INTELLIGENCE SUMMARY.
(Erase heading not required.)

Army Form C. 2118.

Place	Date	Hour	Summary of Events and Information	Remarks and references to Appendices
			located 5 minute later our artillery were shirring on the enemy defences. 2 Artillery officers had crossed the river while our patrol was out. At 20.30 hours on the 8th it was decided to attack and drive the enemy back. The noon and method of attack was as follows. Ptol master Lewis James to have through C.g.b. on front and over by bridge at 1.14 6.8.8 and get into position at C.4.B. LIETARD 19.C. Major TABOR accompanied this Coy and saw the C.O. commanding the unit on our right and explained our attack. This C.O. gave every assistance and supported our Lewis 2 toys to move forward on our right when we jumped our objective. 2 Pl's were ordered to push along road and railway. One Pl. being ordered to mothers up on Pl. was ordered to push every man at 14.C. central. On the centre a division action PLOUY-LECARNÉ and establish themselves on high ground & division section T.B.13Y	

WAR DIARY
or
INTELLIGENCE SUMMARY.
(Erase heading not required.)

Army Form C. 2118.

Place	Date	Hour	Summary of Events and Information	Remarks and references to Appendices
			was sent forward in advance of "B" Coy and to keep in touch with all trains on road to RIVAGE, there being accompanied an enemy post of 3 men near Fayouls and the Coy pushed on and reached from road, the leading section was ordered to race for their 4.8. 2 P+S were ordered to move northwards and push up towards in the direction of HERINNES. 2 P+S Coy our section was to move south, meet up hopes and be in touch with "D" Coy. On the night the advancing Coy ("D") on reaching point 19 centre. They have to fire 2 VERY eights upwards and onwards, the "A" advancing Coy have to do the same when nearing from recess at - 1.3 a 8.3 when their 4.8 knows he knows to have been captured, the same eights were sent up by 6 in H.Q. locations or station 186 with aims to light sent at front, this was the signal by which the Adjutant who was at signal station at Brochehead would know we had forces on Brochen and so	

WAR DIARY
or
INTELLIGENCE SUMMARY.
(Erase heading not required.)

Army Form C. 2118.

Place	Date	Hour	Summary of Events and Information	Remarks and references to Appendices
			inform Bde H. Qrs. Lucas Lowis Mature have established his HB to work back to Brewery at Bridge head in PERG. C'Coy in close support were ordered to send 2 PN's one to E. down Heirles and high ground in 14 a Centres and 2 PN's to junc H.15 and Jenn Tower with N.S.T offs on our left and remainder HERINNES. This was necessary as enemies A Coy advanced in reverse in vicinity of MATLOU at 1.86. Patrols were pushed forward through LE COURROUX in 15 CHEMIN VERT to 16 and toward BOIS de CHIN and GRAND RELIEF. The whole BY was then reorganised and ordered to turn on B Coy as advanced guard. A Coy in Reserve. At 08.45 9-11-18 a hostile machine patrol of 6 by men was observed at JH C7.3 moving NORTHward met the intention of blowing up X Roads, the X Roads at CHIPET were blown up. The patrol was taken off 8 of them being killed. A time was observed on Elefhon from X Roads at JS.6 to J.10 C.7.5 Patrols were at once sent forward in	

Place	Date	Hour	Summary of Events and Information	Remarks and references to Appendices
	19/10/18		The direction VILLAINES - LA LAIE - K8 cent - K2 cent - VILLAINES - LA LAIE - K8 cent - K2 cent. At 06.45 the Bn continued to advance with orders to occupy a line on high ground E of HAUT REVEST E25 d - LA LAIE. A support line was established from E26. c.3.5. K.2.6.8. - K3 cent TRIEUX K10.a - K9 cent. This line was established at 08.15 hours. Patrols were pushed forward in direction of CORDES K46 ANVAING K6 a, FOREST [K1] a. A party of the enemy was encountered and one wounded man of the 7 R. BAVARIAN CAV was found later and brought in by LIEUT CARTER R.A.M.C. The Bn M.O. From information given in. P.S.C.O he advanced to the junction Tom was advanced without item 17 kilometres in a fluid line in 3½ hours without a drop to casualty. Keeping in touch with the enemy the whole time. On roads advance throughout the evening running up many times or 30ody protection new received from B.de 8a at on Junction being established with 89th DIV on left and 29th DIV on right. Fire support was to be withdrawn. The enemy accompanied

WAR DIARY
or
INTELLIGENCE SUMMARY

Army Form C. 2118.

Place	Date	Hour	Summary of Events and Information	Remarks and references to Appendices
	14/11/18		be withdrawn for the 15th and moved to billets in Area D.28. The Coerc'ans have been to renew every arm (Armes and at the request of the C.O fixed a ladder in the road which raised our Archery to fresco as Cluney. At 11 am hostilities were ceased	
HERRIN	15/16/11/18		The B.H. marched back to billets in HERRIN & and remained there till the 16th. The time was devoted to rest and cleaning up and working parties were employed repairing a road and route across the L. of C.'s B.H. proceeded by route march to L.C.Po'x and occupied billets from this date to the end of the month the B.H. refitted, carried out ceremonial parades now more time was given to short practices, men country runs and B.H. and Bell laying competitions in the latter event the B.H. carried off 1st and 17 (Loyal-Lancs) C.S.	

Lieut Colonel
Cmdg 13th Bn East Lancashires
Regt

13th East Lancs Regt

987
40/15

WAR - DIARY

From 1st December 1918
To 31st December 1918

CONFIDENTIAL

Army Form C. 2118.

WAR DIARY
or
INTELLIGENCE SUMMARY.
(Erase heading not required.)

Instructions regarding War Diaries and Intelligence Summaries are contained in F. S. Regs., Part II. and the Staff Manual respectively. Title pages will be prepared in manuscript.

Place	Date	Hour	Summary of Events and Information	Remarks and references to Appendices
Brue	1/12/18		Divine Service.	
	Dec 2		Batln bathing	
	" 3		" bathing & general training	
	" 4		Divisional practice ceremonial parade at NECHIN.	
	" 5		Ceremonial Drill & Companies in attack. Lectures in afternoon.	
	" 6		Company training.	
	" 7		Training under Coy Commanders. Lecture by C.O. in afternoon.	
	" 8		Divine Service.	
	" 9		Skin inspection & Battn Ceremonial drill.	
	" 10		Divl Practice Ceremonial at NECHIN.	
	" 11		Training under Coy arrangements.	
	" 12		Battn Brigade Ceremonial parade.	

Army Form C. 2118.

WAR DIARY
or
INTELLIGENCE SUMMARY.
(Erase heading not required.)

Place	Date	Hour	Summary of Events and Information	Remarks and references to Appendices
CROIX	1918 Dec 13		Batt. Ceremonial Parade.	
	" 14		Started off for Corps Ceremonial Parade - but instructions cancelling parade received when on the march.	
	" 15		Divine Service.	
	" 16		Show inspection & practice Batt. Ceremonial Parade.	
	" 17		Coys inspection at N.E.C.H.N. H.14.d. Sheet 37.	
	" 18		P.T. & B.T. extended order drill. Football in afternoon.	
	" 19		Batt. Route march. Officers riding class afternoon.	
	" 20		P.T. & B.T. & close order drill - football in afternoon.	
	" 21		Platoon Coys in attack - demonstrations.	
	" 22		Divine Service	
	" 23		Route march.	

WAR DIARY
or
INTELLIGENCE SUMMARY.

Army Form C. 2118.

Place	Date	Hour	Summary of Events and Information	Remarks and references to Appendices
CROIX	1918 Dec 24		Commanding Officers Parade. Major Hurd line assumed command of Batt.	
	" 25		Xmas Day - Voluntary Church Service	
	" 26		Boxing Day - Holiday - Sports.	
	" 27		Routemarch.	
	" 28		Close order drill.	
	" 29		Divine Service	
	" 30		Skin inspection. Platoon & Company Training.	
	" 31		Platoon & Company Training.	

J.S.T. Hurd Major
Comdg "13" Saskatchewan Regt.

Army Form C. 2118.

40

13 E Lanc

WAR DIARY
or
INTELLIGENCE SUMMARY.
(Erase heading not required.)

Instructions regarding War Diaries and Intelligence Summaries are contained in F.S. Regs., Part II. and the Staff Manual respectively. Title pages will be prepared in manuscript.

Place	Date	Hour	Summary of Events and Information	Remarks and references to Appendices
CROIX	1919 Jan 1	09.00	Commanding Officer's Inspection	
	2nd	09.00	Battalion Route March about 5 miles then fighting order.	
	3rd	09.00	Battalion Inspected by Major Gen'l at Sir W E PEYTON K.C.B K.V.D D.S.O Commanding 40th Division. In fighting order. Battalion Muster Roll Company Roll, P.R.I. accounts and Books.	
	4th	09.00	Battalion Route March. Drill Order distance covered about 5 miles. Weather wet and very cold.	
	5th	10.45	Divisional Service	
	6th	08.45	A Coy on Range at T.3. and fire practice 5 Rounds application 10 Rounds Rapid. Iron Drill Order with fighting order. Lorries will be carried. Breakfast will be arranged by A Coy.	
		09.30	B. & D. Coys and any available men of H.Q. Coy will parade in HOLDENS FACTORY for P.T.	
		10.00	The above two Coys attended lecture in CROIX CINEMA on League of Nations. Dress. Walking out dress.	

Army Form C. 2118.

WAR DIARY
or
INTELLIGENCE SUMMARY.
(Erase heading not required.)

Place	Date	Hour	Summary of Events and Information	Remarks and references to Appendices
CROIX	Aug 7th		Major The Hon. W.H. LITTLETON is appointed acting 2nd in Command of the Battalion vice Major S. TABOR M.C. to Storr.	
			The weekly S.F.N. inspection took place in HOLDENS FACTORY. D Coy at 11.00 hrs. B Coy 11.20 hrs. C Coy at 11.40 hrs. A Coy at 12.00.	
		07.00 to 11.00	Close order drill by Platoons and Companies	
	Aug 8th		Batt: was inspected by Brig. General. F.P. CROZIER D.S.O. on the parade ground on General General's Inspection	
	Aug 9th		Battalion Baths. D Coy at 8.00 Hrs. B Coy at 11.30 Hrs. C Coy at 9.45 hrs. and A Coy 13.15 Hrs. The Remainder trained with their Coys.	
	Aug 10th		MAJOR The Hon. W.H. LITTLETON assumed Command of the Battn. during the temporary absence of Lt Colonel. H.W.D. COX on leave to U.K. Reinforcement took place this day	L H Littleton Major for H.C. 13th C James Major.

Army Form C. 2118.

WAR DIARY
or
INTELLIGENCE SUMMARY.
(Erase heading not required.)

Instructions regarding War Diaries and Intelligence Summaries are contained in F. S. Regs., Part II. and the Staff Manual respectively. Title pages will be prepared in manuscript.

Place	Date 1919	Hour	Summary of Events and Information	Remarks and references to Appendices
CROIX	Jany 11th		The Battalion paraded for a Practice Parade; at 08.15 Hrs. for the Special Parade Service at ROUBAIX on Sunday for C. of E's. Leave for two were introduced. A Board of SURVEY was held to check the stores of the Batn.	
	Jany 12th		DIVINE SERVICE	
	Jany 13th	09.00	Battalion Parade under Regimental Sergeant Major. Iron ration Issues. — Parade. Companies at Coy. Officers disposal. S/arm Inspection A Coy at 0930 hrs B Coy 09.50 Hrs C Coy 10.10 Hrs D 10.30 Hrs in HOLDENS FACTORY Baths B. Coy 11.00 – 14.00 Hrs Head Quarters 14.00 – 18.00 Hrs	
	Jany 15th		Parades, Guards 08.00 Hrs will parade at 09.00 Hours for drill under Captain B. C. SEYMOUR for practice of parade ground at 09.15 Hours. Remainder of Batn will parade for drill under Reg. Sgt Major. Officers were not to attend this parade.	

Army Form C. 2118.

WAR DIARY
or
INTELLIGENCE SUMMARY.
(Erase heading not required.)

Instructions regarding War Diaries and Intelligence Summaries are contained in F. S. Regs., Part II. and the Staff Manual respectively. Title pages will be prepared in manuscript.

Place	Date 1919	Hour	Summary of Events and Information	Remarks and references to Appendices
CROIX	Jany 16th		Parades. The Battalion paraded in Main Street at 08 15 hrs for practice parade for the Consecration and presentation of Colours to units. Drum was dressed anew with Gloves. Great coats were worn in readiness.	
	Jany 17th		The Battalion paraded again for practice parade for Consecration and presentation of Colours as for Jany 16th. Blankets were dampened.	
	Jany 18th		The Battalion paraded again as for Jany 16th and 17th. 2nd Lt HARROP assumes the appointment of Battalion Canteen Officer	
	Jany 19th		DIVINE SERVICE Rehearsal Parade in GRANDE PLACE ROUBAIX for the Consecration and presentation of Colours. Parade at 08.30 hrs. and marched off at 09.28 hrs.	
	Jany 20th		Battalion Paraded as strong as possible for the Consecration and presentation of Colours in the GRANDE PLACE ROUBAIX by Lieut General SIR HENRY Hon BEAUVOIR DELISLE K.C.B. D.S.O. Commanding XV Corps. at 10.30 hours. Battalion paraded at 09.30 Hours.	

Army Form C. 2118.

WAR DIARY
or
INTELLIGENCE SUMMARY.
(Erase heading not required.)

Instructions regarding War Diaries and Intelligence Summaries are contained in F. S. Regs., Part II. and the Staff Manual respectively. Title pages will be prepared in manuscript.

Place	Date	Hour	Summary of Events and Information	Remarks and references to Appendices
	1919			
CROIX	Jany 22nd	10.00	Battalion paraded as ordered for a lecture by Lt Col PLUNKETT. D.S.O. M.C. on Re-enlistment in the post bellum Army and Reinstatement in civil life	
	Jany 23rd	09.00	Battalion paraded for Route March; also drill order with gloves; distance covered about 3 miles	
	Jany 24th		P.T. and B.F. in HOLDENS FACTORY under Coy arrangements. from 09.30Hrs to 10.30Hrs. Retreat at 17.00Hrs. daily until further notice	
	Jany 25th	0930	Route march. Drill order hem with gloves. Distance covered about 4 miles	
	Jany 26th		"DIVINE SERVICE"	
	Jany 27th		Parades 09.30-10.30 P.T & B.T under Coy arrangements	
	Jany 28th		Cleaning Roads & Saver.	
	Jany 29th		0.93-10.30. P.T & B.T. in HOLDENS FACTORY. under Coy arrangements	
	Jany 30th		Captain A. WALTON. D.S.O. M.C. joined Batt. and posted to A Coy; and extra orders commence WELSH R & T and Pay of Coy	
	Jany 31st		Battalion Baths. A Coy. 09.15-10.30; B Coy 10.30-11.30; C Coy 11.30-12.00 D Coy 14.00-15.00 H.Q and Transport 15.00-16.00	

Confidential.

No 9

War Diary.

13th Bn. East Lancashire Regt.

Feby 1919

Volume IX

W.9

C. Logan. Capt.
13 Bn East Lancs Regt

1/2/19

WAR DIARY
or
INTELLIGENCE SUMMARY.

(Erase heading not required.)

Army Form C. 2118.

Place	Date 1919	Hour	Summary of Events and Information	Remarks and references to Appendices
CROIX	Jan 1		Parade under Coy arrangements. Address for all officers by Divl Comdr in Offrs Mess at 11.30 hr	
	2nd		Divine Service	L.N.
	3rd		All. Coy. Snow-clearing, in area allotted to Battalion	
	4th		Coys at disposal of Coy Comdr	
	5th		Coys at disposal of Coy Comdr. Trip at disposal of Bn Comdr. Special Parade to be paid to Kit-brush.	
	6th		Do. Men Year Honours No 33133 Pte A.H.HARRISSMITH received nomination	
	7th		Baths "A" & "B" Coys at 14.00 hours "C" & "D" Coys at 15.30 hours. All Subaltern officers to report to adjt in Guard Room at 09.30 hrs daily.	
	8th		B" Paraded and marched as Escort to Review Order to Brigade to bid farewell to 5 French 3/10 Inf 5 Regmn 3/8 Pkt of Exchange	
	9th		B" Paraded in Review Order for Ruger's function in St Mihiel	
	10th		Divine Service. B" continued training in Helmer Factory. Issued 1250 × 3 men to report to H.Q. 40 rue Duv Tan.	
	11th		Commenced Brigade Guard Mounting in Square CROIX B" Parade and marched to parade in RUE TROCADERO at 09.30 hr	

WAR DIARY
or
INTELLIGENCE SUMMARY.
(Erase heading not required.)

Army Form C. 2118.

Place	Date 1919	Hour	Summary of Events and Information	Remarks and references to Appendices
CROIX	12th Feb	10.00	Bn was inspected by Brig. Gen. F.P. Crozier D.S.O.	
		11.00	Bn. at ROUBAIX.	
		13.00		
	13th	10.00	Bn. was inspected by Brig Gen. F.P. Crozier D.S.O.	
	14th	9.30	Bn. was inspected by the Comdg. Officer. Transport was inspected by again were the Silver Transport Cup competed for by the 119 Bde Bn. Awarded by Brig Gen. F.P. Crozier D.S.O.	
	15th	10.00	Bn. was inspected by the Comdg Officer. The Bde. sports Bde. boxing competition were resumed the Silver Bugle presented to Brigade H.Q.by 119 Down Service Capt. C. Egan Mordaunt resumed the duties 2nd in Command of the Bn. on from 15-2-19. Vice Major the Hon. H.M. Witaliter who proceeds to 12th Worcester Regt.	
	17th	10.00	The Comdg. Officer inspected the Battalion.	
	18th	10.00	The Bn. Parades as ordered. Parade for Coms & Officers inspection.	
	19th	10.00	The Bn inspected the Bn. after which training was resumed by Battalion.	

WAR DIARY
or
INTELLIGENCE SUMMARY.
(Erase heading not required.)

Army Form C. 2118.

Place	Date	Hour	Summary of Events and Information	Remarks and references to Appendices
CROIX	1919 Feb 20th		The Batts. at ROUBAIX were billetted & the 13th Lowr. Volun.[?]	
	21st	9.15 & 10.30	13th were inspected by the Batt. at 9.30 hrs. Preceded & Holders Lvrs.[?]	
			yesterday Training Billt Football Employment Music & Marching Drill	
	22nd		12 North Staff Regt 2	
			Divine Service	
	23rd		A Bttn emphasis was then upon the continuation Training Specialist Drill	
			Guard Mounting P.T. & B.F.	
	24th		13th Parades for Inspecting by Supt & continuation Training	
	25th		The regt was issued with Stocking Cape and new Pattern	
	26th		large wire cut disposed of by Coy Comdrs for cleaning & hauling etc	
			equipment	
	27th		13th Who inspected by G.O. at 9.30 hrs Bns. Battle order without	
			Steel-helmets.	
	28th		13th were inspected by the Regt at 9.30 hrs. Training continued	
			till midday	

1st Battalion
East Lancashire Regt

13th Br East Lancs Regt
Vol 10

War Diary

Volume X

For Month of March 1919.

W.10

Army Form C. 2118.

WAR DIARY
or
INTELLIGENCE SUMMARY.
(Erase heading not required.)

Place	Date	Hour	Summary of Events and Information	Remarks and references to Appendices
CROIX	March 1st		13th Paraded at 9.30 & were inspected by the Adjutant. Evening continued until noon.	
	2nd		Divine Service. Summer time came into use at 23.00 hours	
	3rd	09.30	Bn "Army of Occupation" Men paraded for inspection by Adjutant.	
	4th		"Army of Occupation" Men were inspected by Adjutant.	
	5th		Baths at ROUBAIX were allotted to the Bn.	
	6th		Inspection ushered/finished(?)	
	7th		Draft of 11 Officers & 76 Other Ranks proceeded to 1st/5th Bn of regiment. Remainder of Bn were formed into two Coys.	
	8th			

Army Form C. 2118.

WAR DIARY
or
INTELLIGENCE SUMMARY.
(Erase heading not required.)

Instructions regarding War Diaries and Intelligence Summaries are contained in F. S. Regs., Part II. and the Staff Manual respectively. Title pages will be prepared in manuscript.

Place	Date	Hour	Summary of Events and Information	Remarks and references to Appendices
BOIX	9		Divine Service in English Schook at 10.00 hours.	
	10		Usual training	
	11		Infantry training	
	12		Battalion Rousta attached to B?	
	13		Usual training	
	14		Do	
	15		Do	
	16		Divine Service English School hour 10.00 hours	
	17		Divisional Commander visited from & inspected type to Brigade on appointment to Command a Division Lieuten to the Rhine.	
	18		Usual training	
	19		Do	
	20		Do	
	21		Do	
	22		Do	
	23		Divine Service in School Room at 10.00 hours.	

A6945 Wt. W14422/M1160 350,000 12/16 D. D. & L. Forms/C/2118/14.

Army Form C. 2118.

WAR DIARY
or
INTELLIGENCE SUMMARY.
(Erase heading not required.)

Place	Date	Hour	Summary of Events and Information	Remarks and references to Appendices
Corbie	August 24		Moved forward	
	25		Battle at Morlancourt above objective to 13".	
	26		Moved forward	
	27		Do	
	28		Do	
	29		Do	
	30		Do	
	31			

O/C Record Section.
British Troops in France

Herewith A.Fs. C.2118 for month of April 1919
please

[Stamp: 13TH EAST LANCS. REGT. No. L237. Date 10-5-19]

G. Clapham Lieut & adjt
13th B'n East Lancashire Regt

Army Form C. 2118.

13 E Lanc

WAR DIARY
or
INTELLIGENCE SUMMARY.
(Erase heading not required.)

Instructions regarding War Diaries and Intelligence Summaries are contained in F. S. Regs., Part II. and the Staff Manual respectively. Title pages will be prepared in manuscript.

Place	Date	Hour	Summary of Events and Information	Remarks and references to Appendices
CROIX	1/4/19		Usual Training.	
"	2/4/19		"	
"	3/4/19		The G.O.C. [Brigadier General S.P. Rosrgur] D.S.O.] inspected Baths Establishment, Football Ground across Canal 9.30.	
"	4/4/19		Usual Training:	
"			No. 2 Bade Group Sports Meeting. Result 13th East Lancs Regt. 1st.	
"	5/4/19		Usual Training	
"	6/4/19		DIVINE SERVICE	
"	7/4/19		Usual Training	
"	8/4/19		"	
"	9/4/19		Baths at Roubaix 10.00 – 11.00 hrs	
"	10/4/19		Usual Training	
"	11/4/19		"	
"	12/4/19		"	
"	13/4/19		DIVINE SERVICE	

Army Form C. 2118.

WAR DIARY
or
INTELLIGENCE SUMMARY.
(Erase heading not required.)

Instructions regarding War Diaries and Intelligence Summaries are contained in F. S. Regs., Part II. and the Staff Manual respectively. Title pages will be prepared in manuscript.

Place	Date	Hour	Summary of Events and Information	Remarks and references to Appendices
CROIX	15/9/19		Baths 10.30 – 11.15 Roubaix.	
	16/9/19		Usual Training	
	17/9/19		"	
	18/9/19		"	
	19/9/19		"	
	20/9/19		"	
	21/9/19		DIVINE SERVICE Usual Training	
	22/9/19		"	
	23/9/19		Baths Roubaix 10.00 – 11.00 hrs	
	24/9/19		Usual Training	
	25/9/19		"	
	26/9/19		"	
	27/9/19		"	
	28/9/19		DIVINE SERVICE	
	29/9/19		Baths Roubaix 10.15. – 11.00 hrs	
	30/9/19		Usual Training	

TEL. 84 LUTON.

note 29.1.25
vii

13ᴬ

30, STUDLEY ROAD,
LUTON, BEDS.

14. XII. 24

My dear Major General,

I am in receipt of General Pearce's letter also one from Colonel Pinhorn, re East Lancashire Regt War diary and shall be very pleased to

render any assistance in my power.
I have a very few War maps which
I shall look up and send to you.
Would you like me to go to the
Historical Records Office and get a few
records from the War Diary of the 13th
Bn. or has that been arranged for?

Yours very sincerely
Sidney Tabor Major

P.S. So sorry I could
not come to Regtl dinner.

TELEPHONE:
1305 READING.

Armand
24.1.25

Bn
13

BLANDFORD LODGE,
WHITEKNIGHTS,
READING.

24.1.25

Dear General.

I see that you are compiling a War History of your Regt. For the last 7 months of the war I had one of yr Battns in my Brigade (119th), 13th I think it was or if not 13th then 12th.

These men came to me as B.1. men in May 1918, but from July to the end of the war they fought, marched & behaved like quite class A men. Their extraordinary effort is I think deserving of special record. Their Colonel (R.S. Andrews DSO & ...) has since been unfortunately killed in an accident, but he had an astonishing grip over his men. He had served with me from 3rd Bn to Lt Col, from Feby 1917. On almost the last day of the war 8/9th Nov, I believe, these so called

P.S.
[marginal note, vertical:]
Our dead
recovered
& buried
at Mortier
in the Tank
Yesterday's
the war,
burial
at Laghi
Recd & read
M.C.
Rooties
Evening
Telegram
3 bivouacs
near Lines

B.I. men crossed the Scheldt on
improvised rafts, pushed back
the German rear guard & marched
many miles, thus demonstrating the
fact that the 'A' standard is
dependent entirely on where the
heart is situated. The Btn was
given 10 miles in that day's work
& 2 or 3 officers got the M.C., among
them Major Tabor (acting 2 i/c R!)
who is a member of the Stock
Exchange & whose keen brain would
assist you in your work of
compiling. Please excuse me for
"backing in" but I owe a lot to the
doings of the Btn & of ye Regt, which I
can never hope to repay.

Yours truly
F. P. Crozier
Brig. Gen'l

ALBEMARLE COURT HOTEL.
(Under same Management as Hotel Commodore, Pembridge Square, W.2.)
LEINSTER GARDENS,
LANCASTER GATE. W.2.
3 minutes from Tube, Bus and Hyde Park.

PHONES (2 LINES)
PADDINGTON 7228-4419
TELEGRAMS.
"APPORTER, LONDON."
ELECTRIC PASSENGER LIFT
TO ALL FLOORS.

Gas Fire and Phone in every Room.
Hot and Cold running water.
Central Heating.

12/9/27

Dear Sir Lothian,

Enclosed typescript from Tabn. 13/Batt'n.

Hope you are going strong.

Kind selaams.

Yours

H. P. [signature]

P.S. I hope all the rest is coming in.

P.S.(2) What do you think of the London Branches Scheme for a Supper Party?

HISTORY OF 13th. Bn. THE EAST LANCASHIRE REGIMENT.

After the debacle of the 5th Army in 1918, one of the Divisions the 40th, known as the Bantam Div, who made a great name at Bourlon Wood, and had suffered such heavy losses in April 1918 that it was found necessary to reform and build up a new Division again, the Labour Corps were called on to supply drafts to the 9 Bns. of which the 13th Bn. East Lancs was one of these Bns, were first called garrison Bns., of which the 8th Bn. received the name of the 13th East Lancashire. The first formation took place of Bn. H. Q. at ETAPLES on June 18th 1918 with Lieut Col W. Hodson D.S.O.M.C. in Command, Cheshire Regt. Major S. Tabor, Bedfordshire Regt. 2nd in Command and Capt. J. W. Stopford, Bedfordshire Regt. as Adjutant. On June 11th Colonel Hodson was ordered to join 35th Division, Major Tabor assumed Command.
On June 16th, 17 Officers and 760 O.R. arrived at WATTEN to form the four Companies, the Bn. formed part of the 119th Infantry Bde. under Brig. Genl. F. P. Crogier D.S.O. who in later days commanded the Black & Tans in Ireland. Lieut. Colonel R.I.B. Johnson, D.S.O., R.W.F., took over Command. Division General at this time was Major General Ponsonby who soon left to Command the 5th Division and was succeeded by Major General Sir W.E.Peyton C.M.G. who retained Command of the Division till demobilized in June 1919.

As a number of Officers and men had not been in the line for some time and a great many never had, it was necessary that they should be put into strict training in the neighbourhood of ST. OMER and later at HAZEBROOK where they had a lot of training in forming an outpost line, for at this period the character of hostilities had changed to a more open character. The Bn. by this

time had been through a severe course of training, and
on July 17th went to Reserve near METEREN where the
Australian Bde. in conjunction with the 9th Div. had
carried out a most successful operation.   The Bn.
went into the Line on the night of July 22nd and 23rd at
STAZEELE holding an outpost position on the right of
the Australian Bde. facing CELERY COPSE.   Active
patrolling was carried out and a few prisoners captured
whose password was Hamburg; they were evidently looking
for a sausage and got collared.   A raid was carried
out on the night of the 25th on an enemy outpost,
unfortunately Lieut. Mason A.I.F., and his Corporal who
were on lookers were killed.   The raiding party went
back and recovered their bodies.   During the first
tour in the line the Bn. was attached to the 1st.
Australian Div. who placed at our services one Officer
and 4 N.C.Os. to each Company, as they having been in
this section for some time knew it well.   This was
most useful and a great friendship struck up, as both
Colonel Johnson and Major Tabor were themselves
Australians born.   The Bn. was relieved and went
into Hazebrook finding guards working parties etc, and
generally fitting themselves for next tour in Line.
This included a week at LUMBRES for musketery.   The
Bn. showed great improvement.   The practices on last
day were witnessed by General Sir H. Plumer K.C.B., who
congratulated the Bn. on their display of fire discipline.
The Bn. was now in good trim for another tour, and went
into the Line at VIEUX BERQUIN on the night of August
22nd, relieving 24th Bn. R.W.F.   This sector was a
very important one, as the enemy's Artillery had got every
likely position taped.   A Bn. [Coy] was holding an
outpost line, reliefs were difficult.   On July 27th
the 13th Bn. R. INNIS. FUS. 120 Bde. carried out an

attack on BECKET CORNER supported by the 13th Bn. East Lancs. The attack was successful. Unfortunately our L.G.O. Lieut. H. N. Carter was killed, and our Adjutant Capt. G. S. Stopford was wounded. The Bn. took over the position and it was quite evident that the enemy were firing off dumps, as their fire was so heavy, which proved to be correct, for they retired at 10.p.m. on the night of the 28th. Relieved on the night of July 30th. During the two tours in the Line in VIEUX BERQUIN Sector, the Bn. came under heavy shell fire and gas. Total casualities. Officers 6 O.R. 95.

After a period in reserve the Bn. again went in the Line to man the NIEPPE SYSTEM of trenches on the NIEPPE -ARMENTIERS ROAD on August 6th covering a front of about 6,500 yards. This was a wide front to hold, however, orders were received that an attack should be made on PONT NIEPPE, the object being to establish posts on the River LYS. The attack was made at 10 a.m. on Sept. 6th under a lifting barrage. A & D Companies were detailed for this operation. D Company kept close up to the barrage and gained objective without casualities, and endeavoured to establish connection with a Bn. of another Bde., but this Bn. had failed in their objective and at dusk we were ordered to withdraw. D Company were held up by M.G. fire and sniping from ruined houses, and were in danger of being surrounded so wisely retired. The attack on the whole was highly satisfactory, as valuable information was gained as to the enemy's position. Total and strength of the two attacking companies was only 105. Considering the heavy losses inflicted on the enemy, our casualities were slight for this operation. Three Military Crosses and eight Military Medals were awarded.

The Bn. went into support on Sept 8th at LEETS FARM. On the night of Sept. 12th C. Company sent out a fighting patrol Lieut. C.A. James objective crossing River LYS at PONT NIEPPE, but were unable to cross as the river was in flood, and the remains of bridge having been washed away, no doubt destroyed by enemy who retired after heavy bombardment from all calibres after our attack on the 7th. Total casualities 1 Officer 42 O. Ranks.

On Sept. 13th, went into Bde. reserve at PONT WEMEAU, and later at HAZEBROOK area for general training fatigues etc. On Sept. 26th the Bn. was moved by train to BAILLEUL. Oh what a change from the dear little town some of us knew in the early days of 1914-15, when one could get a whisky and soda at the FAUCON; help yourself for 50 centimes. Now all ruins. The writer had a billet then recently evacuated by Genl. VON KLUCK. On the night of Sept. 26 the Bn. under the Command of Major O'Connor 13th R. INNIS. FUS. took up an outpost line in the NIEPPE SYSTEM liason posts established with 31st Div. and 121st Bde. Active patrolling took place and the objective was to cross the River WARNAVE. At night two strong patrols went out and three bridges were slung across the River. This was successfully carried out when the whole Bn. advanced and established a new Line on the 30th. Patrols pushed forward by day, were held up at times by M.G. and Rifle Fire. This was overcome and Bn. was relieved by night of vanguard duties by the 13th R. INNIS. FUS. Total casualities in this successful operation was 9 killed 54 wounded and 18 missing. October 4th the Bn. was moved up in support over the River LYS, N.E. of Armentiers. Lieut. Colonel Andrews D.S.O., M.C, late C.O. 17th S. W. Bn. the Welsh Regiment joined the Bn. and assumed Command. On October 7th from this date to the 18th, Bn. was training

and moved by route march and occupied an old enemy camp. and was specially detailed from 19th to 21st and worked on the railway near LILLE between PERENCHIES and STANDRE. The Bn. stopped and relaid 5 kilometres of railway. The Bn. moved by route march to BONDUES - ROUBAIX, acting as advance guard to brigade and attacked BONDUES. This was done as an exercise. The brigade was moved to WATTRELOS less the Bn. who went to CROIX, and worked again on the railway under the Canadian Rly. Corps, for some days. On October 27th the Bn. attended Divine Service at the French Church in CROIX by special request of the Cure on the freedom of the Town, and also at the English Church where the small British Coloney of 50 souls had been all through the war, and had not had meat for two years, the result being the Bn. Head Quarters had to go on short rations for a few days. Mr. Metcalfe, 70 years of age, the Manager of Messrs. ISAAC HOLDEN the pioneers of wool combing in ROUBAIX told us many interesting tales of how he managed to hide a great deal of copper in the works from the enemy, and his wife was the daughter of the late Chaplain who had held the position for 50 years. The Bn. rejoined the Bde. on the 28th at WATTRELOS, excellent billets, the inhabitants of both sexes were most obliging, in fact the Padre and M.O. were lost for three days, having managed to find a most select billet. The 2nd in Command thought that the Bn. Head Quarters would be better for their health. For a few days the Bn. was busy in practising platoons in the attack on strong points, as we were shortly going to a rather nasty spot namely PECQ, where we relieved the 23rd Bn. Lancashire Fus. on November 4th. PECQ is situated on the ESCAUT. The River here is wide and the bridge having been destroyed, the only means of crossing was by a plank footbridge which was often washed away owing to heavy rains.
Bn. Head Quarters situated at CHATEAU in ESTAIMBOURG.

Active patrolling by day and night was carried out along le RIVAGE.   One N.C.O. killed and 3 O.R. wounded.   On November 5th we attempted to push over the ESCAUT.   2nd Lieut. CHATTERTON D.C.M., with his platoon crossed lower down by an old enemy pontoon bridge, and got in touch with 11th Bn. SOMERSET L.I.   He was held up for a short time by the enemy M.G., this was successfully dealt with.   At the same time 2nd Lieut. McLELLAN with his platoon advanced along le RIVAGE to try and capture a strong post in a crater.   This was strongly held and we were heavily trench mortared but were able to locate and find out the enemy's trench.   Our casualties were only slight. Another attempt was made by two platoons, one on each side of le RIVAGE causeway, and succeeded in getting quite close to crater which they bombed with grenades and smoke bombs. Under orders they retired and came under heavy M.G. and mortar fire.   The floods were very heavy now, men having to wade through two or three feet of water.   On November 6th and 7th the whole Bn. front, including Bn. Head Quarters came under intensely heavy fire of all calibres, principally 8".   We had several casualities from gas.   At Bn Head Quarters alone there were direct hits and gas masks had to be worn for two hours.   Our friends the gunners came to see us, expecting to find the Chateau on our heads, as the enemy's fire had been so intent and accurate.   We, however, gave them an excellent breakfast of eggs and bacon which the Head Quarter's Cook had to cook, in his mask.   During these days we had been massing all calibres of artillery, as our ~~Div.~~ Commander, General de LISLE, had decided on a heavy bombardment to assist our attempts to get along le RIVAGE. On the 8th we decided to make an attack.   A daylight patrol was organised by C.O. and was sent out with orders to draw enemy fire, then retire.   This was successfully accomplished.   At 20.30 hours on 8th Lieut. James with his Company D., accompanied by 2nd in Command, Major Tabor had orders to pass through 59th Div, Front on our right and cross by bridge at 1.14 b 8.8.   The C.O. Commanding Unit here explained, gave every assistance and sent us two companies for support.

When we gained our objective 2 PNs were ordered to push along road and railway, 1. PN being detailed as moppers up 1. PN to establish themselves on high ground at PLOUY-LE CARNE 1.4.C. Central B. Company in centre passed over LE RIVAGE and bayoneted an enemy strong post and reached HERINNES. D. Company on right reported by VERY lights that they had occupied HILL 48 where they were joined by C. Company the Bn. was reorganised and ordered to push on at 08.45.   On 9. 11. 18 a hostile mounted patrol was met and disposed of leaving three killed.   A line was established at CLIPET from X roads at J. 5C to J 10. C. 7. 5.   On the 10th the Bn. had orders to advance and occupy a high position E. of REJET LA LAIE.   A small party of enemy were encountered and one wounded man of the 7th BAVARIAN CAV was found and brought in by our American M. O. Lieut. Carter. M.C. R.A.M.C.

From jumping point in PECQ the Bn., advanced 17 kilometres in 32 hours keeping in touch with the enemy the whole time. Junction was established with the 29th Div. on left and 59th Div. on right.   Our advance had been very rapid, and Corps Commander General de LISLE could not believe we had advanced so far, and as we were pinched out were ordered to retire.

11th Nov. hostilities were ceased.   The Bn. were then in good billets at CHATEAUX de BRUYERE at PAS CELLES after a few days here Bn were ordered to proceed by route march to take billets at CROIX en ROUBAIX where they remained till demobolised in 1919.   While at CROIX the Bn. refitted and did a good deal of Ceremonial drill, sports such as football, cross country runs and boxing.   In the latter event the Bn. carried off 5 events out of 7 in the X th CORPS.

www.ingramcontent.com/pod-product-compliance
Lightning Source LLC
Chambersburg PA
CBHW081531160426
43191CB00011B/1735